30: A Sense of Adventure and No Sense of Direction

30: A Sense of Adventure and No Sense of Direction

Copyright © Mark Callaghan 2008. All rights reserved.

Visit the author's website at: www.thirty30.co.uk

ISBN 978-1-4092-1819-7

First Printing: July 2008

Acknowledgements

Thanks to the following people who all played a part in this shambles finally making it to print: my mother, who, no matter where I am in the world or what sort of mess I've managed to find myself in, manages to offer assistance in a calm and considered fashion (even if she's tearing her hair out at the time). My brother John (whose artistic talents know no bounds) for the cover work and various other creative favours. Nigel, who helped get the writing piece underway; Faith Ann Carroll and Anastasia Cassella-Young, for turning my babble into comprehensible English and Mike Smith for making it all look like a book rather than a bucket of words emptied onto paper. My uncle Terry, who always provides me with a cold beer, good food and a bed whenever I land in Australia, thirsty and penniless; Miriah & Dave, for being a huge help during a horrific few days in Buenos Aires; Nic 'Bradders' Bradley and Emma 'Ferret' Perrett, for the time, energy and enthusiasm they put into launching the book; the state museum in Oswiecim; Tuol Sleng museum and anyone else that managed to stay interested over the two long years it took to finally make this book a reality.

For Kim

Introduction

I recall with some clarity the moment I knew that I didn't want to sit in an office and dream up inventive ways of wasting time until 5pm any longer.

I'd made my way into the building fashionably late and winked cheekily at the receptionist who I had a bit of a thing for (she sneered and whispered something that sounded a little like 'nobhead'). I dumped my coat, switched on the laptop, checked my voicemail for messages, decided there was nothing interesting enough to keep me from my breakfast and hit the cafeteria for a fry-up and a caffeine hit. On returning, I checked the football news and loudly hinted to anyone within earshot that I quite fancied a nice cup of tea, in the vain hope that someone may volunteer to make me one. When this didn't seem to be forthcoming I made my way to the toilet.

Now, I know the last thing you want to hear is what went on in said toilet but please bear with me here. After a short game-playing session (playing computer games on your mobile phone whilst sitting on the toilet is a surefire time-wasting winner - not many bosses will feel comfortable broaching the subject of how long you spend on the toilet in the morning), I experienced something of an epiphany. Needing to share my revelation, I waddled from the men's room with my trousers round my ankles, pointed my finger to the sky, announced to anyone within earshot that things were about to change, waved my tie like a lasso and hurled it into the nearest shredder, pulled up my trousers and sprinted out of the office.

I came back in of course. But what had dawned on me was that I needed to get away - and right away. I'd spent a year doing the now compulsory Brit pastime of backpacking Australia and New Zealand back in my mid-twenties - people would once marvel at the fact that you were adventurous enough to 'go all the way down under' but now so many have been to the aforementioned 'down under', that we all know it's a one year piss-up in a sunnier, happier version of the UK doing a few odd jobs to keep a roof over your head. I began to consider how I was going to conjure up a trip that would both inspire and challenge me...

The '30' idea was born from several different conversations. It wasn't a secret that I was approaching thirty in a few month's time (no one would let me forget it), and I had been looking for an original idea to mark the occasion for a while. My circle of friends (is three people enough for a circle?) had been discussing doing something different to celebrate, but I was looking for something truly memorable and, after a brief moment of enlightenment in the bath (seemingly all my greatest ideas come when either I'm washing or on the toilet), decided that it would be good to make the trip in conjunction with my birthday.

The money saving began in earnest whilst I waited for the final pieces to slip into place during hygiene breaks. These 'light bulbs' arrived shortly after: firstly, in a conversation with a female friend who told me she wanted to visit every country in the world and us attempting to work out how many there were to get around and secondly, after telling another friend that I was going travelling again, her suggestion that I should "write a book about it, your stories are funny" (actually, she may have said "utter nonsense" but that's by the by). That was the point when I formulated the theme of the 'challenge': to travel thirty countries, beginning on my 30th birthday, and then write a hilarious book of my experiences.

Choosing the thirty countries was a surprisingly speedy affair; I knew that they would need to be cheap to travel, relatively safe (i.e. not in the midst of a civil war) and easily reachable in conjunction with my proposed flights. I bought two, cheap flights in and out of Europe, one into Estonia in the East and one out of Portugal in the West. This allowed me two months to cover half of the thirty countries, overland, using trains & buses. I then purchased a 'round the world' plane ticket (with the help of my faithful credit card) with ten flights, which would cover fifteen remaining countries across three more continents. Simple.

After much number-crunching, it became apparent that my 'rainy day' savings didn't come close to covering the estimated cost of the trip and, even with a sizeable (aren't they generous folk?) limit on my credit card, I was going to need some more cash. With less than two months until the off, it was time to get things moving. Even with working all the overtime permitted (which wasn't much) and staying in as much as humanly possible (only going out for special occasions - such as William Shakespeare's birthday), much more money was required. Things needed to be sold.

So it was that any item I owned that didn't have sentimental value was fair game. I became a committed 'E-Bayer' and watched as my personal belongings sold for anything between highly inflated and next to nothing. I got sick to the back teeth of packaging everything up and driving to the post office on my lunch break every other day to send it out. I sold my PC to a workmate's son, and then had a moment of horror when I realised there was a chance I hadn't deleted some choice adult material from it. Even after all this I still didn't make the target figure - the rest would just have to be borrowed and worried about some other time.

The weeks soon passed; my possessions dwindled and as it slowly dawned on me what I was doing, everything began to click into place. I'd chosen the countries, the flights were booked and I'd drawn up a basic (and what was to turn out to be a completely un-realistic) itinerary to try and keep me roughly on track time and money wise. I dug out my old, faithful backpack 'Clive' from the loft and, after a brief catch up, started to work out how I was going to fit the extensive list of equipment I'd made into a space that small (answer: I wasn't). I was immunised against every disease known to man (several I'd never heard of) and began to cancel all those direct debits and contracts that keep you tied down wherever you are (one of the most enjoyable activities you can ever undertake).

I received a surprise call from my travel agent at work, just four days before I was due to leave. She explained that I couldn't have my round-the-world air ticket, as there was a problem with one of the flights being over-booked (it was something like that,

I'd begun to sweat profusely and was having a panic attack of sorts so was having difficulty concentrating) - they were therefore cancelling the ticket. I spent my last two days of work scrambling around trying to find a replacement ticket. In the end, I could only find one with fewer flights and had to purchase individual tickets direct from several airlines to fill in the gaps. I was also left a country short: Fiji had been lost (from the trip, not off the map) and was hurriedly replaced by Ireland.

And that was it. I had a low-key, lunchtime send off from work (I don't think I was very popular) and on exiting the building, was struck by that strange mixture of elation, excitement and absolute fear you experience when you walk away from a job knowing that you've just voluntarily given up your career (if you had one) to start afresh. The tune that played on my car radio as I drove out of the car park will stick with me forever; I still smile when I hear it today.

And the book? It's a collection of some of the most memorable stories from the trip. Written with the aid of my notes (which, due to my appalling handwriting and tendency to write after I'd spent the night sampling the local hospitality, may not be entirely accurate), my slightly fuzzy long-term memory and my inclination to visualise situations as comedy sketches in my head rather than accept the bland (or dangerous) reality. I don't profess to being an expert in history, art, geography, architecture or politics (although I'm fairly knowledgeable on 1980's TV shows) but will always attempt to fill you in if I felt it had a bearing on my state of mind at the time; it's mostly an account, from my slightly warped perspective, of what I saw and what happened to me and memorable individuals I met, as some serious 'Turbo Tourism' swept me across four continents in nine months. I hope you enjoy reading it.

Oh, there is just one more thing - should reading this make you walk out of your job and embark on a similarly hair-brained scheme, then please don't tell your loved ones that it was anything to do with this book - I really can't handle that kind of responsibility.

0.5 - Clive

I have a habit of naming things I own. I think it's because I don't have any friends. It's not that I make friends with things I own, you understand (that would be ridiculous) - I just name them. That way it gives me someone to blame when something goes wrong.

My backpack is named Clive. I can't recall why, you can't really go back and change someone's name once they've got it though, can you?

As an aside: my flip-flops are named Chas and Dave.

1 - Estonia

Hostels & hostel life

Now seems like as good a time as any to give you the low-down on hostels. This type of accommodation will more often than not serve as my 'home' during the trip and they're a little different to your 'Holiday Inn' or 'Vera's Bed & Breakfast' (they don't have coffee sachets that went out of date six years ago or black and white televisions that can only receive BBC2).

A very basic hostel will normally consist of some shared sleeping rooms (usually in bunk beds, ranging in number from 4-40 to a room), sometimes with lockers for your valuables (other times you'll need to come up with an ingenious hiding place that no would-be thief would think of searching – your pillowcase for example), shared bathrooms (toilets, showers – normally individual compartments and sinks), some type of communal lounge area and a kitchen for cooking your meals (pasta being the number one backpacker's choice for several years running). Of course, all hostels vary greatly in terms of size, comfort, cleanliness, amenities and most importantly – atmosphere. With budget world travel becoming ever more popular, hostels are known to have bars (the bar is more important than the hostel in some cases), Internet cafés, TVs and DVDs, swimming pools, huge welcoming communal areas, help with finding work, saunas, gyms and even the occasional crèche if you wish to bring your child along with you and leave them in qualified hands whilst you gallivant around the globe for a year. Probably.

My first ever night spent in a hostel (one recalls it with great nostalgia) was four years previous in Cairns, Australia, and it set a high standard for barmy nights in dormitories. I was sleeping off my long flight from the UK (and a few opening night beers) when a skinny Scottish lad in his late teens burst through the door in a state of severe drunkenness. I watched with one eye open as he staggered across the room and finally crashed into his bed. The nights were cold (for Australia) at this time of year and our Scottish friend obviously hadn't packed a sleeping bag, he lay shivering and fidgeting, his teeth chattering, before suddenly bursting into tears. I was about to show my concern for his well-being but, before I could, he sprang to his feet, ran out of the room, stopped a few feet outside the door and relieved himself on the corridor floor outside. He then returned to bed, put some more clothes on, had another cry and fell asleep. When I awoke in the morning, eager to question him about his behaviour, the bed was empty and nothing was left of the lad apart from a nice, big patch of piss outside our door.

Anyway, I digress. Having touched down in Estonia's capital Tallinn, the hostel at which I've arrived, on the outskirts of the old town, is one of the smallest I've ever laid eyes on. In essence, it's a studio apartment that's being utilised as crowded, shared accommodation. The reception area is a small desk in the cramped entrance hallway and a door opens into the rest of the hostel. The all-in-one rooms are the kitchen, living area and 3 bunk beds. Another slightly more private dorm lies in an adjoining room (but it's full) and there is one toilet and a shower room (the fact that this shower room contains a decent spa bath and a sauna convinces me that this place wasn't designed as a hostel). The people are friendly enough though, and I'm not planning on spending an awful lot of time here, so I throw Clive onto an empty bed to claim it as my own (as is the tradition). I prefer a bottom bunk if possible as it's far less hassle during the night; I've seen some nasty 'top bunk' drinking injuries in my time I can tell you. It's funny how I've shifted from the childhood school of thinking that claiming the top bunk is a pre-requisite whilst rooming with a younger brother/schoolmate, to opting for a lower bunk in my later life for my own personal safety.

Another major aspect of hostel life is meeting strangers. Before you leave for a solo trip, one of your concerns is always 'am I going to meet people?' – That may be one of the reasons you're going away after all. The answer is normally 'yes' (with a little effort on your part). Hostels are always geared up to meeting people, as there's really no other option. Pretty much every area of the place is communal so you'd find it tough to be alone, unless 1) you make a concerted effort to, or 2) you're the only person in the hostel – then you're in trouble (try hooking up with one of the cleaners – works for me).

A shocking first night

I will remember the first night of my trip for a long time. Not with any fondness I'm afraid, but because I was stuck in an uncomfortable situation. Still feeling a little tender from my boozy farewell the previous night, I'd disinterestedly picked at my dinner in a nearby bar with two American lads - a likeable young student and a sleazy, overweight grease ball. Estonia has more than its fair share of beautiful women, and my slimy, lard bucket of a companion has taken it upon himself to make a lewd comment (coupled with a snort) every time one passes us by. After deciding that I really don't want to spend any more time in the company of this irritating ogre, I return to the hostel. My fragile condition soon takes a turn for the worse and, before long, I find myself kneeling on the toilet floor 'talking on the porcelain telephone'. Being the only toilet in the hostel and slap-bang next to the communal area, this means that all in the living area are well aware of what's happening. After a good hour of loud vomiting, I emerge as a flaky ghost to some seriously funny looks (and a queue of miffed people waiting for the toilet). As I fall wearily onto my bunk, the sweats arrive and, as quickly as I can remove a couple of layers of clothing, the shivers are on the scene. All I can do is wrap up as warm as I can, close my eyes, curl into a ball and try to ignore the noise in the communal area around me. It's still early, maybe 10pm; the TV is blaring out 'The Simpsons' at full blast, someone is crashing around in the kitchen (it sounds as if they're trying to prepare a meal blindfolded) and a girl nearby is packing and re-packing her bag over and over again (how can one bag have that many zips?) - I assume she has a stopwatch and is attempting to beat her packing/re-packing personal best.

All this combined made for a miserable night. Unbeknown to me, it doesn't seem to get dark in Eastern Europe (at this particular time of year anyway) so the window by my head lets in the semi-dark evening light whilst I intermittently sweat and shiver. Individuals return to the hostel during the course of the night and every sound is amplified in my head. At one point during the peak of the fever, madness sets in and I decide that I'm going to walk home to England and scrap the whole trip. Fortunately, the need to vomit again means that I don't have to follow up on the logistics of this bright idea.

When I open my eyes the following morning, I'm surprised to find myself back in my bunk bed as the last thing I remember was nodding off whilst hugging the toilet for comfort. Other than still suffering from a lack of sleep, I don't feel too bad. I figure I must have had one of those 'twenty-four hour bugs' that people talk about – I'm unaware if there is an official medical name for this illness, but I'd be awfully surprised if it's professionally recognised as the 'twenty-four hour bug'.

The Bog

I'd taken a bus south from Tallinn to my next port of call: Estonia's summer capital – Parnu, pre-booking a night at a hostel in nearby Soomaa, which is apparently around half an hour away. Soomaa is famous for its bogs (in fact I seem to remember the name actually meaning 'land of the bogs' or something along those lines) and outdoor activities.

The buses out to the village where the hostel lies are infrequent to say the least, and most of the day has already passed by the time I manage to touchdown in Soomaa and locate the hut that will serve as my accommodation for the night. It's an odd looking place, I'm not sure whether it doubles up as the community centre for the small village, but there's an old theatre of some kind, circa 1960's decor and the place seems to be full of young children who aren't staying there but are using the facilities. There's no one at the reception when I eventually locate it through the swarms of kids, and it takes me a while to locate an adult (I don't know if you've ever seen the 'Children of the Corn' film, but I was beginning to get the feeling that this tiny outpost had been overtaken by murderous children and was considering making a run for it). Eventually I locate someone taller than waist high who works at the place and, after going through the formalities, I'm shown to my dorm. I find that the entire place is empty. I'm the only person staying here. Those bloodthirsty children have murdered all the other travelers. Possibly.

After informing the chap at reception that I think I'll just stay for the one night, he kindly organises some cheap accommodation for me in Parnu for the following night and asks what I plan on doing for the remainder of my day.

"How about some canoeing?" I suggest. He then informs me that, as I'm the only person staying here, I'd have to pay an extortionate amount to go canoeing.

"Right, OK, what do you suggest then?" I ask.

"You could go and walk the bog," says he, and explains that there's a plentiful supply of bog to walk around - this one in particular being a 5km trail. He offers to drive me over there but explains he won't be around to bring me back so advises that I'll have to return by my own devices. Now, I've never been to a bog before so figure 'why not' and jump in his jeep. I must have missed the bit where he said that the bog was 6km away; I ask him if there's a bus I can get back. He informs me that there's no such thing and my choice is either to walk or hitch a ride; I decide to cross that bridge when I come to it and thank him for the lift.

I make my way into the bog through a huge, wooden wishbone and begin to stride along the wooden planks that guide the way along the trail; allegedly witches can be found in the bogs, as they enjoy the isolation. I keep an eye out for black-cloaked, green-skinned, cackling women with pointy hats, but all I see is bog and more bog. Although I'd been told that there are areas in the bog in which you can swim, I'm unsure of swimming in a location that may be rife with witches, so I remove my shoes and dip my ever-tired feet into the cool water and listen for the sound of broomsticks. Whilst I'm soaking my feet and reviewing the pros and cons of my snap decision to walk around a bog, a frog begins to croak, and is quickly joined by a few of his mates, the croaking continues to multiply until there must be over a hundred of them making one hell of a din. I'm reminded of 'The Frog Chorus' by Paul McCartney and join in with a couple of cheerful 'Bay-ee-aas'. The frogs aren't at all impressed at my gate crashing their party and stop instantaneously. I sigh; feeling a little left out, and continue walking the planks.

After what seems like hours, I finally finish the circuit, arrive back at the beginning and am then hit with the realisation that, after walking a 5km trail of nothing but planks/bog/singing frogs, I now have to make my way 6km back to the hostel. I scan the dirt track road for any sign of traffic; it's deserted, so I reluctantly set off toward the village — at least I think it's the track toward the village — I must admit I wasn't really paying attention when I was given directions. I've still got that bloody frog song bouncing round my head and find myself singing it as I'm walking along. I try to wash it out with another tune and somehow end up with 'I would walk five hundred miles' (which I wouldn't, I'm having enough trouble with 6km). After around fifteen minutes of ambling down the road singing to myself, a dusty white car pulls up alongside me and the driver beckons me in. I happily accept his offer as a ride rather than a kidnap attempt and we're on our way. The driver, a friendly middle aged fellow, is nattering away in Estonian to me and at first I smile blankly before realising that he may be pitching some questions my way, so I let him know that I can't speak Estonian. It becomes apparent from his body language that he wants to know where I'm heading (makes sense I suppose, that's normally what happens with hitchhiking). That's all very well, except I have no idea/clue what my hostel is called. I throw a few words and hand signals intended to indicate hostel, bed, accommodation and sleeping but, understandably, he has absolutely no idea what I'm talking about. I recall seeing a shop nearby and offer 'shop?' He nods knowingly. I really hope he's thinking what I'm thinking; otherwise I'm going to end up very lost in the 'land of the bogs'. With luck it's the very one. I thank him for his kindness and walk the short distance remaining to my 'hostel for one'.

2 – Latvia

First night in Riga

I take the bus down into Latvia from Parnu, I'd heard that Riga was a 'party city' (hence it being an Eastern European stag party hotspot) and that most of the hostels were fairly social affairs – the one I'd selected certainly was. A blackboard in the common room recommends the liveliest establishments for each evening and the best time to get there. At 10pm a large group of backpackers from all over the globe excitedly congregate in the common room and we notice that we've unintentionally formed our very own stag party – there are no women. After visiting a couple of the city's bars we make our way to a place named 'Fashion Club' - a stylish affair which has a long catwalk running down its centre surrounded by a bar. We've been told there's a nightly fashion show so, as an announcer appears from behind the curtain and barks out something in Latvian, we all mill over to the catwalk to take in the proceedings. Unfortunately for us, 'the show' involves a group of orange-skinned male bodybuilders, wearing nothing but far-too-tight red Speedos, parading down the runway in a publicity stunt for those sickly rum 'alcopops' that girls like. As luck would have it, one of the muscle bound posers decides to douse himself with booze in (he thinks) a seductive display for the whooping ladies in attendance, when the unlucky chap bounding energetically down the catwalk behind him slips up in slapstick cartoon fashion on the combination of booze, fake tan and baby oil, landing with a huge thud on the catwalk - cue rapturous laughter.

Around an hour later the curtain opens again – 'This must be the women!' we cheer, shuffling over to the catwalk once more. Enter a Latvian fellow in a suit (who looks a little like 'Sloth' from 'The Goonies') playing some kind of demented 'turbo violin' to techno music and whacking himself in the face regularly because of the ridiculous speed at which he was playing. What a surreal place.

Latvian trampolining

I soon find that it's difficult to avoid the party scene in Riga (to be fair, I didn't try very hard) and the next few days whiz by in something of a drunken haze: evening drinks at beer tents whilst listening to local bands, unwittingly (honest!) finding myself in an expensive, upper class strip club policed by some of the scariest looking Russian bouncers I'd ever laid eyes on (tip to hostelries – employ bouncers that look like they'll snap your neck if you ask where to find the toilets – you'll find that occurrences of trouble will rapidly decline), finding an abandoned, bemused 'stag' standing lost in the middle of the street wearing only ugg-boots and a pair of tiny comedy y-fronts, discovering that our hostel has CCTV in the secluded internet room when one of the lads gets a little amorous with a girl in the early hours and is applauded by hostel staff the following morning after his performance was witnessed by the night shift. Having a civilized, sit-down pizza meal at a respectable restaurant at 5am after stumbling out of a nightclub and discovering it was broad daylight (I'm not convinced it ever got dark) and lastly, coming across the world's greatest busker – an elderly woman, possibly as old as eighty, dressed in her Sunday best (including a fetching hat) and dancing to hard trance music. What a town!

My final night in Riga was spent in much the same fashion as those previous, early evening soaking up the atmosphere at the beer tents and then onto various bars before a club. Some hours later, I happened out into the daylight with a friend and ambled into a nearby park where, in our boozy state, we were delighted to find an un-attended (it was very early in the morning) group of trampolines. As you'd expect, after some cheering we excitedly climbed on board a 'tramp' each. We were just about to begin our 'routines' when a voice called out in English from underneath: "You have to pay". Just as we were discussing the modern wonder of speaking trampolines that can request/accept payment, a disheveled, tired looking man crawled out from underneath. It transpired that he'd been sleeping down there and was either a) working the night shift at the trampolines and taking forty winks whilst guarding his livelihood against pissed up, irresponsible tourists, or b) a tramp. Whoever he was, we paid him handsomely and commenced our trampolining. I returned to the hostel minutes later with ripped jeans, a strained neck and a possible broken ankle.

3 – Lithuania

Vilnius – speaking Lithuanian

I hop on the bus again, traveling from Riga to Vilnius - Lithuania's capital city. During the uneventful five-hour trip, I discover that the rugged guards on the Lithuanian border would make for fine nightclub doormen: tough-looking and bloody miserable. On arrival at the bus station in Vilnius, I'm greeted with the tune of 'Shaggy' (the reggae guy, not the dude from Scooby-Doo) showing 'the nation his appreciation' (it was a recording you understand, 'Shaggy' wasn't performing a gig at Vilnius bus station), which was a bit of a surprise. It would be nice if it caught on though, imagine being welcomed by shitty pop music every time you arrive at your destination – a sure-fire winner.

I don't have any accommodation booked and it's getting dark quickly so I'm becoming a little concerned. I'd scrawled down a couple of addresses of youth hostels and the icy welcome I receive from an un-smiling female receptionist at the first place I try convinces me that this is the hostel for me. As luck would have it, they have one bed left for the night. A few smiles and a bit of banter thaws the ice queen out a little and we're soon the best of friends (she stops making throat-slitting gestures at me).

After the standard introductions of name, country of residence and where you've been/where you're going, I join my roommates for a few warm-up beers and a plan is hatched for the evening: one of the group, a charismatic American chap named Dylan, has recently purchased a rather unhelpful Lithuanian phrasebook that contains some downright useless sentences. We decide to learn one useless phrase each and pledge to try them out on the locals during the night ahead.

We head to a bar/club that is spectacularly 90's in every way: the décor, music and even the way people are dressed (it may have even been a 90's theme bar - I'm really not sure) make me feel like I've jumped back fifteen years – except I'm not wearing an avocado coloured suit or polo neck, my hair isn't cut into a 'step' and I don't have severe teenage acne (I have to rush to the bathroom to confirm all this). We have a couple of the local brews and then my American friend informs me that he feels it's high time to try out our newly-learned Lithuanian. We approach a couple of friendly looking girls and get to work:

"My name is Cucumber Envelope," announces Dylan, introducing himself with a cheeky smile. OK. Just confused looks so far. He nudges me, and looks toward the baffled locals.

"Erm, I've lost my son," I deliver in seamless Lithuanian.

"You've lost your son?" One of the girls replies in perfect English - with a concerned expression.

"Uhm, Yeah. Yeah," I nod, worrying where this conversation is now likely to lead following my false revelation of both fatherhood and the loss of my imaginary child.

"When did you lose him?" - Her concern at the situation grows

"Erm, maybe a week ago?" – An answer that's not likely to help this uncomfortable situation

"A week ago! How? Where?" – She's absolutely horrified, this joke isn't quite progressing as we imagined...

I know of only one way to prevent this tomfoolery spiraling out of control... "I have to go to the toilet" - You genius Mark

On resurfacing some minutes later, I decide that 1) I'm not going to attempt any more of the lingo without learning something useful and 2) I'm not going to go anywhere near the girl who I was talking to about my lost son, as she's now throwing me some serious daggers (dirty looks I mean – she wasn't angry enough to throw knives at me) across the room. I briefly consider approaching her and trying to explain my fictional son and his part in a hilarious ruse but the inevitable, complicated conversation that will follow doesn't seem worth the effort. The fact that a grinning 'Cucumber Envelope' has got off scot-free is also difficult to stomach.

Some time later, after hitting the dance floor to the sounds of 'Snap' and 'Blackbox', a beautiful, yet frightfully drunk Lithuanian girl slumps on a chair at our table and stares at us for ten minutes without uttering a word before staggering off to freak another table out. I'm quite drunk and tired by this point so decide this is a good juncture to head back to the hostel where the next morning one of the lads has an interesting story to tell about a girl he left the bar with last night. She'd invited him back to her place and, at some point during the night (I'm not aware at which point), informed him that a) she was married and b) her husband was a bodyguard for the president of Lithuania - suffice to say he didn't stay much longer.

Funnily enough, it also transpired that the girl in question was the very same girl who showed such great concern for my fictional lost son – just who is she to cast aspersions on my fathering skills? - The brazen hussy.

4 – Poland

Moving On: Vilnius to Warsaw

As the bus pulled away from Vilnius bus station, I was unable to make out which song was bidding me farewell. I'd like to think it was 'Chakademus and Pliers' singing 'Tease Me'. I wave a cheerful, energetic farewell to a man and his dog waiting to cross the street and a look of complete bewilderment spreads across his face. The driver puts the radio on and it's blaring out some cracking, accordion-based music. He's straight on the microphone and blabbers something in Lithuanian or Polish, maybe even Russian – I would guess that it was the rules of the bus but he could have been introducing himself as 'DJ Tomas' and letting us know that if we had any accordion based music requests, then to make our way to the front of the bus and let his assistant 'Kelly' know. The silly man forgets to turn off the microphone and places it by his gear stick, the reason I know this is because once the music is turned off to allow the passengers to try and get some sleep, all you can hear is the sound of him changing gear over the speakers. I wish I knew what the Lithuanian, Polish or Russian lingo for 'turn off the microphone' is – I don't think telling him that I've lost my son is going to solve this issue.

At 2am we arrive at the Polish border and a slightly less scary guard than normal boards the bus, collects everyone's passports and disappears into a small building nearby. After a long, silent wait in the dark, the bus pulls off to universal panic (in several languages) from its passengers. No one has had their passport returned. It transpires that they're all sitting nicely on the drivers lap and the 'take-one-and-pass-it-down' method is being employed on the pitch-black bus. I end up with a Russian passport and try and swap it for a more exciting one, getting my own one back in the process. Slightly disappointing, but I decide to go with it.

Meeting the 'Frat Boys'

After spending a day walking the streets of Warsaw and finding not an awful lot of interest (apart from a massive tower of monstrosity named the 'Palace of Culture & Science'), I return to my hostel to find that I am sharing my dorm room with a group of three American 'frat boy' types – this is apparently a nickname given to American lads in their early twenties who attend college and like to drink and 'party hard'. I was unaware that this type of person existed outside of the movie world before traveling Europe, but discovered in time that there are more than enough of them to go round (three each to be exact). From what I can gather at first glance, although they seem educated and relatively well spoken, they do have a habit of speaking loudly, swearing loudly, regularly swapping quotes from their favourite films (loudly) and doing a lot of shouting, back slapping and 'high-fiving' when they find anything they agree on (as well as that tilted handshake where you go in with an arm wrestling type grip). I'm interested to see how these guys interact outside in the real world so, when they introduce themselves and ask me if I fancy going out for a beer, I accept with a round of 'high fives' and some whooping – all in the name of research of course.

We take part in a pub-crawl organised by the hostel (I quickly discover that one of the frat boys has incredibly poor social skills and should be locked away for his own safety – I nickname him 'liability') and I'm pleasantly surprised to find that Warsaw has some decent bars and clubs. I have a good night: I lose the Americans at some stage, find myself doing the 'running man' on the dance floor of a sweaty warehouse club, unsuccessfully attempt to speak to a pretty Polish girl using broken French (I'm not sure why) and find myself alone in the middle of an unfamiliar, deserted street at dawn. As luck would have it, 'the Palace of Culture and Science' stands tall in the distance and guides me home.

Checking Out

The next morning I stay in bed as late as I can before I'm obliged to checkout. Backpacker hostels have wildly differing checkout times and routines (vacating your bed, locker and any other facilities you may be using) – usually between a friendly (and very welcome) midday and the downright nasty (and feared) 10am checkout. Bring your bed sheets to reception for washing, leave 'em on the bed, wash your bedding before you're permitted to leave, bringing the whole bunk to reception for a thorough steam clean – different places, different rules. Some of the more laid back places don't really have any rules around checking out (or any rules at all for that matter) and won't sell your bed to someone else until you finally drag yourself out of it at three in the afternoon and tell them you think you might be leaving but you're not really sure.

Moving On: Warsaw to Krakow

I make my way to Warszawa Centralna train station – it's absolute bloody mayhem. I sidestep a shouting drunk, give an apologetic shrug to a squadron of beggars setting out toward me and take my place in the lengthy queue at the ticket window. A Scandinavian girl who had obviously been having trouble at the window comes away shaking her head and stating that 'no one in Poland speaks English'. I hastily prepare some handwritten notes and practice my hand signals to ready myself. An angry old man ambles up to the queue shouting and pushes in at the front; the chap he's shoved in front of takes exception and a shouting match ensues, with the old man victorious following a fine display of aggression. A teenager taps me on the arm and asks in English (see – some people do speak it) if I can give him money for his grandfather in Krakow. I explain that I'm not looking for a grandfather at the moment but if the situation changes can he leave his card and I'll give him a ring. On reaching the window, the woman behind it tries her utmost not to help me but I'm too well prepared and patient. She soon gives up and sells me a ticket to Krakow (which, fortunately, is where I wanted to go).

I'd been looking forward to roaming around Europe by train and this was to be the first of many journeys. I excitedly locate my compartment and find that it's the size of a shoebox (for a very small pair of shoes), and was full. I show my ticket hopefully and fortunately, someone gets up to leave. I now have myself a seat but need to tackle the problem of where to put Clive: the paltry luggage racks are full and there is no space on the floor. It's a frazzling 32 degrees outside and inside the box is a damn sight warmer. After a failed attempt at re-shuffling the luggage already on the rack I slump to my seat, dripping with sweat and reluctantly wrench the heavy Clive onto my lap. An elderly gent sitting opposite kindly suggests I place Clive on the floor and we both rest our feet on him. I don't need asking twice and as the train pulls off do just that. I thank him very much and notice that his shirt is unbuttoned; revealing a large, sagging belly and his fly is undone - displaying some discoloured underpants. I'm unsure where to look, so I glance at the fellow next to him who is sporting a magnificent, bushy mono-brow. He catches me staring in marvel and I flit to the skinny, attractive female sitting by the doorway - she gives me a dirty look. I dig out a book to read.

Krakow – The Frat Boys return

Shortly after arriving at my hostel in Krakow, the American frat-boys arrive (I think I must have unintentionally mentioned where I was staying) and they've already been on the booze throughout their train journey. I've become something of a cult figure with them (they think I'm funny for some reason) and they ask me along for some food and a few drinks – I decide to go along as a minder more than anything else, concerned what harm they may come to. What followed was certainly interesting. After several beers I realised that none of them know how to behave in public – you may be able to get away with swearing, wrestling, whooping and throwing drinks at one another down at your local bar in Austin, Texas (or wherever) but behaving in this style in Eastern Europe is likely to get you in to a world of bother.

As the evening wore on, it became apparent that one in particular (the chap I'd affectionately dubbed 'liability') was going to be great trouble. We'd descended into a cavern style club with a labyrinth of rooms. It was hot, sweaty and smoky and I cringed when I saw that two of the lads had taken a table in a crowded seating area. Within moments, 'liability' had barged into a member of a stag party on his way back from the bar and was now getting some seriously funny looks. He started chatting up other men's girlfriends, spilled his drink (and everyone else's) over their table and had mistakenly elbowed a large Irish chap who looked like he was going to crush our friend's head with his bare hands – of course, he was oblivious to the whole thing. I decided as much as staying here would help my research (and possibly make for an entertaining anecdote), that being mistaken for a frat boy and taking a good hiding from a group of pissed up rugby players wasn't on my agenda for the night (that's tomorrow). It later transpired that 'liability' had surprisingly been ejected from the club shortly after and, in an attempt to find his way home, trudged five kilometers out of the city, realised he had absolutely no idea where he was and booked into a hotel for the night.

Anyway, Krakow is a wonderful city to visit. It has a historic old town with cobbled streets, a decent nightlife and the summer weather is warm but not too overwhelming. The frat boys were still sleeping off the effects of the previous night and so I was free to roam the streets on my own without having to break up any fights, apologise to bystanders or whoop any high-school football team names (Go Wildcats!). I walk down to the vast town square which is bustling with activity; I pause to watch a group playing traditional music and am about to applaud the fine work of the lead accordion player (nothing like a good accordion solo), when I discover that Krakow is home to a crack squadron of suicide pigeons. The first one brushed the top of my head but the second is headed straight into my face and I throw myself to the floor before sprinting into the Sukiennice (Cloth Hall) – a building that dominates the square and has a marketplace that runs underneath it. I inspect the wares on offer – including plates, jewelry, shitty t-shirts and swords. I ask a stallholder how much he's asking for a sword as I picture myself charging from safety and giving the pigeons a taste of their own medicine, but decide this would probably lead to arrest and detention, so forgo the idea.

I poke my head out of the safe haven and notice that a group of kids are entertaining tourists and pigeons alike with a moneymaking break dance routine. I see this as an ideal diversion and venture up to the Barbican which used to surround the principal gateway into Krakow and was an important defence point in the Middle Ages: It has turrets where, if you're a skilled archer, you can pick invaders (or tourists) off at will. I wouldn't say I'm particularly skilled, but do manage to hit a man selling postcards in the neck - which I'm quite happy with.

An Unwelcome Addition

I'm absolutely horrified to find that three has become four when I return to the hostel after my days sightseeing (and a couple of cold beers) - we have another frat boy in our midst. The new addition is a lanky, brash, opinionated guy (let's call him 'Todd') and he's already throwing personal insults around – this despite the fact that he's wearing a bright yellow shirt. I'd already decided on a night in, as I'm getting up early in the morning to go to Auschwitz and want a clear head. Whilst I'm eating my dinner (pasta of course), 'Todd' is challenging anyone he can find to listen to him (which is very few people indeed) into a drinking competition to show everyone what a top fellow he is. After convincing absolutely no one to join him, he undertakes a solitaire drinking game, drinks himself stupid and becomes even more obnoxious than he already was. He finally leaves after smashing what little remains of a bottle of vodka on the floor and calling anybody who didn't want to spend the rest of the evening in his charming company a 'homo' – what a special guy.

I discover that night that you observe a lot more happening in a dorm room when you're sober. Unless you're a strong sleeper (which I'm certainly not), you notice the people getting up to go to the toilet, those returning from partying at 3/4/5/6 o'clock in the morning and the enormous, bearded Canadian hippo-man who snores like a trooper. I vow never to go to bed sober again - this could be the start of a nasty drinking habit.

Auschwitz

The next morning I go to the train and bus station (for they're in the same place) and enquire about traveling to Auschwitz (Oswieciem) - I'm accompanied by the frat-boys. The town of Oswieciem is 75km from Krakow and it transpires that we've missed the train, and so need to take a bus; I'm directed to a nearby window where, after some language difficulty, I walk away with a ticket. We wait around for a bus with a swelling crowd and, as soon as one arrives, everyone swarms to squeeze aboard. We push our way on and show our tickets; the driver sternly shakes his head and points us off the bus. We're incredulous at this and ask him why but he doesn't speak

English. The people behind us are shoving to get on but we're keen to know why we're not allowed to travel. Our total inability to communicate with the driver means tempers begin to fray; a man interrupts at just the right time and explains that the reason the driver is pointing us off the bus is because we're trying to use a train ticket to get on – he then relays the story to those already on the bus. After the laughter subsides, we pay for a bus ticket and sheepishly move down the vehicle. The frat-boys are laughing and joking and making me slightly nervous about the prospect of visiting a concentration camp with them - I isolate myself from them, taking a seat some way away. After a two-hour journey, the crowded bus pulls up at Oswieciem train station where it's a short walk to the museum.

Auschwitz is, without a doubt, the most upsetting place I have ever visited in my life. As soon as I walk through the notorious gate, surrounded by barbed wire fencing and bearing the lie 'Arbeit Macht Frei' (work brings freedom), a horrible feeling grows in the pit of my stomach and the more you see, the more you struggle to believe that something this horrifying could actually have taken place. The first prisoners arrived here in 1940 and you are shown the buildings that the prisoners were kept in, the inhumane conditions they lived in, the slave labour that they were forced to endure, torture cells, a wall where prisoners were executed (now covered with wreaths and flowers), gas chambers and furnaces. Most hauntingly, seeing on display the piles of suitcases, shoes, spectacles and hair kept by the Nazis really makes you realise how huge this atrocity was.

Three kilometers away is the second part of Auschwitz – Birkenau. This vast second camp was where mass exterminations took place and was added to the original complex in 1941. It contained nearly 300 barracks, making it the largest part of the complex – it was here that the Jews arriving from all over Europe had to face a selection process. After arriving by rail, at the platform, anyone deemed to be unfit for slave labour would be sent directly to the gas chambers - this included the ill, the elderly, pregnant women and children. In most cases, 70-75% of each transport was sent to immediate death.

Some of the wooden barracks that housed those who were allowed to live are still standing and they are testament to the awful conditions they had to endure. In 1944, with the Soviet army advancing, the Nazis began an attempt to destroy evidence of the crimes they had committed: documents were destroyed and buildings dismantled. The huge gas chambers and crematoriums lie in ruins at one end of the camp but the train tracks that lead into the complex still remain. The sheer enormity of the place and the haunting view of those tracks leading toward the site of the gas chambers create a vision of what a huge, appalling operation the Nazis carried out.

The memorial at Birkenau sums it up as well as can be possible:

'For ever let this place be a cry of despair and a warning to humanity, where the Nazi's murdered about one and a half million men, women and children, mainly Jews, from various countries of Europe,
Auschwitz-Birkenau 1940-1945'

Normally when you've witnessed a distressing exhibit in a museum, you can feel your mood lighten somewhat once you exit into the daylight but here that's not the case – you're in the midst of where it actually happened and it's all very troubling. The crowds waiting for the infrequent buses back to Krakow are growing out of control and I spot a private minibus pull up some way down the street. I run over, ask the driver if he has any space and we come to an agreement to buy a seat. My head is heavy and I'm not feeling great about the world, so I end up on a major vodka session, awaking the next morning with a very thick head.

Buying a beer

I'd bumped into two friendly American lads who were a touch more refined than the frat-boys the previous evening, and we were hatching a plan to head for the Czech Republic on a train this very night. Unfortunately, our cocky American amigo 'Todd' has overheard our conversation and wants a slice of the action.

The three of us end up hiding in a corridor nearby, forming a huddle and rehearsing a sketch that involves us staying in Krakow one more day, moving hostels and not leaving until the following night which, when acted out in front of Todd, is very believable – I was particularly pleased with my performance (playing myself).

There's just time to grab some fast food and a beer before we head to the train station and I stroll into a pizza place, order my food and check out their fridge to see what beer they have to offer. There's a beer that we've been drinking called 'Zywiec' so I ask if I can have one of those (pointing) – "a 'Zvike' please!" My pronunciation couldn't have been quite spot on though, as the girl at the till has a stifled giggle. I make another attempt – 'Zwike?' and this time she just laughs - as well as one of the guys making the pizza whom I notice gives a very accurate impression of me to his mate who also cracks up. One of the Americans, who was perusing the menu nearby, overhears the commotion and comes over. I explain I'm just trying to order a beer but am having a little trouble with the pronunciation – "I've tried 'Zvike' and 'Zwike' with hilarious consequences" I say, nodding towards the studio audience who are struggling to regain their composure. He confidently requests a 'Zveek' – the three members of staff erupt and one collapses to his knees clutching his sides. After the girl behind the counter finally wipes away her tears she presents us with two beers. As we make our way outside, the door closes behind us and we hear the laughter breaking out once more. The worst thing is I have to collect my pizza twenty minutes later and, after a brief period of calm when I arrive at the counter, it becomes apparent that the two 'chefs' are having real trouble keeping it all in and, before long, they explode into raptures of laughter once more.

The Train of Terror

The train from Krakow to Prague is alleged to be Europe's most dangerous night train. Stories circulate the backpacking community of entire compartments being gassed: rendering the inhabitants unconscious and their belongings stolen, muggings, pickpockets, ritual sacrifices and a man on horseback riding through the carriages beheading passengers with a rusty sword (I may have made that last one up). We excitedly walk down to the train station and set about buying some tickets. After queuing at the ticket office we're faced by an altogether unhappy woman whom we inform that we want to buy a ticket for the train to Prague tonight. She wants to see our passports – we haven't brought them of course and have to get a taxi to the hostel and back.

On our return, we queue once more and meet the same po-faced woman – we're better prepared this time and, as well as our passports, we have the times of the two trains that we're interested in. We show the lady and she explains that all the sleeper compartments on the first train are reserved, leaving only seats available, and the second train doesn't exist. We reply that we're not keen on sitting down on the 'train of terror' and want to be safely tucked up in bed in a nice locked compartment please - is she sure that the second train doesn't exist? We've just got it from a timetable? She shrugs disinterestedly and nods to a different window across the way, which is for information; she just sells tickets and doesn't give information you see.

To cut a very long story short, we visit the ticket and the information window alternately another three times, as the two women flatly refuse to communicate with one another. The ticket lady will only sell tickets and the information lady will only give information. Finally, after what seems like hours of negotiations, the ticket lady begrudgingly admits that the second train does exist but there are only first class sleeper compartments left.

"Do they have a lock?" We ask.

"Yes," she replies.

"Then we'll take one," we say, with a huge sigh of relief.

We catch a train to Katowice, which is where we'll connect with our overnighter to Prague. A drunken man with a yellow cape and a silly hat runs down the middle of the train shouting - I assume he's the conductor. Katowice train station is a grim place indeed; we have an hour wait here and, after paying for a pricey visit to a disgusting toilet, I fall over a tramp that's made his bed in the entrance. He offers me some cardboard and a tempting sleeping position next to him but I politely refuse. I escape the smell of urine emanating around the ghastly place, walk up to the platform and eagerly await the 'Train of Terror'.

The 'Train of Terror' ominously pulls in to Katowice station and we jump onto our specified carriage, hurriedly locate our compartment and I nervously keep watch along the corridor whilst the other two arrange their belongings before ducking in and locking the door. The compartment is clean and comfortable, with pillows and sheets on each of the triple bunks and a fine, secure lock. We each consume several shots of vodka for courage and I take the precaution of adding some extra barricades, a couple of booby-traps and blocking the bottom of the door with a blanket to prevent gas being sprayed underneath - we brace ourselves for imminent attack.

It transpires that apart from a fairly grueling journey, the only scary moment comes when I sleepily (or drunkenly) stumble from our compartment (after spending half an hour removing our traps/barricades) to the men's room barefooted and piss on my feet. Nightmare.

5 – Czech Republic

Cesky Krumlov is a stunning little medieval town in the south of the Czech Republic - you instantly warm to the place, its well kept cobbled streets, the brightly painted, old, red-roofed buildings, petite shops and the picturesque surrounding countryside, forest and river Vltava which hugs the town's edges.

On checking into our hostel, we're told that we've come on the right day, as it's free beer today - the hostel holds a barbeque and provides a keg for all staying there – superb timing! We struggle to haul our packs up a set of steep wooden steps (actually it's more of a ladder) into an attic dormitory, and are surprised to find quite a different type of living area to the norm. It's a loft with wooden floors and pillars, filled with countless single beds and washing lines packed with clothes hung across the rafters. Even more mattresses are squeezed in on platforms up in the roof to make for maximum money earning potential. The scene reminds me of Fagin's place in 'Oliver'.

'Rafting'

Cesky Krumlov is something of a haven for backpackers and one of the reasons for its popularity (as well as being a lovely place and providing free beer) is being able to take a raft down the river Vltava. The basic premise is that you hire a big rubber dinghy, fill it with five or six people, take a load of beer and then make your way from the drop-off point back toward the town.

We hire two rafts and have a real mixed bag of nationalities on board – two Brits, two Americans, and four Norwegian girls, an Aussie, a Kiwi and a Canadian. After realising that using the oars provided to paddle 1) took far too much energy and 2) made very little difference to the speed and direction of the vessel, we decide to just kick back and enjoy the scenery. We drift through the tree-filled hills that sandwich the river, floating through the town itself, greeting fellow rafters and kayakers with 'ahoy!' (At least that's what I thought it was), leaping aboard rival boats and 'borrowing' some of their alcohol when our supply inexplicably runs dry.

We experience the occasional twinge of excitement from a tame 'rapid', I hog a rope swing downriver watched by a school party who wish I'd stop playing the arse and get off so they can have a go, at the same time realising that the reason the water is 'lovely and warm' is because there's something that looks like sewage pumping into it. Our progress is slowed by constantly having to stop at the side of the river and negotiate the jagged rocks underneath the surface because everyone can't stop pissing after consuming too much beer. We're ravaged by mosquitoes as the sun starts to go down and it dawns that we've set a snails pace and are going to miss our collection time by a long way (but we still pause at a random caravan selling hot-dogs at the riverside because most of the group have the munchies). A tired attempt is made at rowing to make up some time, but this is abandoned after ten minutes of going round in circles. We finally arrive at the rendezvous point very late and in near darkness to cheerfully greet the extremely unhappy raft guy.

Absinthe

Cesky Krumlov has some wonderful restaurants perched on the bank of the river and a few of us stop by in the evening to have a meal outside on the decking (for your information I have a fabulous steak). As soon as I begin to remark on the lovely surroundings it starts to piss down with rain and we have to retreat inside. The remainder of the night is something of a blur, as I was introduced to the phenomenon that is 'Absinthe'. Absinthe (as I understand it) is an incredibly strong alcoholic herbal drink, green in colour. Apparently, you're not supposed to drink it using the 'Czech Method' which involves soaking a spoonful of sugar in a shot of Absinthe, then setting it alight (melting the sugar) before plunging it back into the glass (once it's no longer alight) and then drinking the contents in one. Whether you're supposed to drink it this way or not, that's what everyone was doing and who am I to argue? Anyway, after a few (possibly five) of these, all I can recall is going to a warm, lively pub and returning home* some time later by bouncing off the buildings in a pinball style before realising that the hostel was over-full. The reason I'm able to make this statement is because someone was sleeping on a mattress on the floor of the already overcrowded dorm. As my brain hadn't programmed this piece of furniture from earlier in the day into my 'drunk map', I tripped on said mattress and sprang into bed with an extremely scared looking girl. I apologised for the intrusion, tried explaining that I hadn't programmed her in, knocking her out with my breath before collapsing onto the correct bed, discovering that the hostel was spinning and falling unconscious.

* It's amazing how quickly a place (any place) can become considered as your 'home' whilst you're on your travels. All you may have is a wooden bunk bed amongst a cramped sixteen-person dormitory with one filthy shower between the lot of you, but when you stand in that hot (or freezing) shower and fall on that (lumpy) bed after a long day traipsing around a city or an obscene journey, it feels like you're home. Well, sort of.

I have to checkout at 11am the next morning. I try to make an argument with the front desk that the availability of absinthe locally should allow for a far later checkout time but they won't budge. I feel awful and, after downing my bodyweight in water, try to fill my insides with some goodness to turn this horrific hangover around. The best I can find is a fruit salad, so I force that down and, along with one of my American buddies, head for the bus to Prague (the other one loved the place so much he wanted to stay – either that or he couldn't get out of bed from the absinthe hangover).

Toenail Clipping

Prague: I have an entertaining experience in the hostel shower room which has some rubbish sensor operated lights installed. If you're not showering vigorously enough (and I'm a pretty vigorous showerer I'll have you know) the room goes pitch black and you have to wave around in front of the sensor like a maniac for the light to come back on again. After far more dark and waving than I would choose to have during a shower, I make for my room and am welcomed by the rear view of a very large girl in her bra and quickly disappearing panties. I'm a little taken aback by the scene before me but sit on my bunk, mind my own business and go about clipping my toenails into a carrier bag (I was unable to perform this ritual in the shower room as it kept plunging into darkness and I didn't want to lose a toe). The 'curvy' American girl suddenly pipes up and complains that my toe-clipping is a little anti-social in a dorm environment. I'm not sure whether it's any more anti-social than a semi naked whale whose knickers are being swallowed by her enormous backside so I clip on regardless.

Kutna Hora

It's Sunday lunchtime and we're planning to travel to the town of Kutna Hora (70 km from Prague) to visit a church made out of human bones (as you do). The train timetable is pretty scant today and, after a lot of fannying around, we don't manage to get on a train until the early afternoon. This doesn't leave much time to make it there, see the sights and return. On arriving at Kutna Hora train station I'm walking along the subway underneath the tracks and am greeted with a slogan proclaiming 'Fuck Disco' in bright red paint – I wonder if we'll have time to check this disco out later on.

It transpires that we only just have time to visit the Bone Church (the Ossuary), which strangely enough is a very old chapel that has been decorated inside with the remains of 40,000 dead people (they died in a plague in the 14th century apparently) rather than a 'church made out of human bones' as I had imagined. The small building's interior is filled with bone sculptures, bone coats-of-arms, bone pillars and even an ornate chandelier which contains every bone in the human body - delightfully oddball. It's a spooky little place I can tell you.

We hastily walk back to the station to catch the train back to Prague and I notice a poster advertising a 'James Bond 007 night with Lesby Show' – I consider staying to witness what should be an interesting night (especially with the possibility of a trip to the Fuck Disco afterward) but know I have precious little time left in the Czech Republic. On boarding our train, we sit next to a fellow sporting a pair of tiny denim hot pants, a silver beard, pony tail and a screaming loud Hawaii shirt – I never wished I could be someone else so much.

6 – Slovakia

As the train tickets were so darn cheap, I treat myself to a first-class fare from Prague to Bratislava. And may I say what a lovely, comfortable journey it was. We raced through fields of green, yellow and brown and I smiled contentedly as I lazed in my spacious seat and flitted between snoozing, getting some well-needed writing done and chatting to a lovely pair of Italian sisters.

I arrive in Bratislava feeling completely relaxed and something feels good about the city; I'm welcomed warmly at the hostel and it's a beautiful sunny day. After spending the afternoon sitting in the sun, people-watching at a nearby café, I return to the hostel and am delighted to meet an 84-year-old Italian lady who is backpacking Europe alone armed with little more than a fierce temper and a cane. Everyone takes to her instantly and she becomes known around the hostel as 'Grandma' (and to a lesser degree 'Supergran').

After fixing dinner (pasta) I accept an invitation from a couple of the 'hostelers' for a spot of weed outside. It's been quite some while since I'd smoked weed and a few minutes later I remember why I stopped. After drinking several litres of water to combat my extreme cottonmouth I make my excuses and go for a lie down in a dormitory that was spinning a lot more than I remember. I snooze for an hour or so and on awaking (and drinking a lot more water), am kept awake throughout the night by assorted disturbances: 1) terrible Eurovision music booming out from a nearby bar 2) loud drunks singing (badly) 3) some clown changing his bedclothes at 3am 4) extreme paranoia from aforementioned weed (I seem to recall preaching aloud during the night but am unsure whether I imagined this or not – I really hope I did) 5) some thoughtful workmen attacking the road/building outside my window at seven o'clock in the morning.

The next day had been earmarked for sightseeing but I discover it's a public holiday and everywhere is closed, making the city a ghost town. Yesterday's sun and warm temperatures have disappeared and, as I make my way outside, the conditions shift from overcast to blustery to light rain and finally gale force winds - resulting in windows being smashed around me as I walk. I shelter at the tourist information office and try and find something to do today - preferably inside.

I walk up to Bratislava Castle, which is known affectionately as 'the table' (because it looks like a table). There isn't an awful lot to it and to take refuge from the elements I spend some time in the castle museum. Now, I'm sure an exhibit on antique furniture will get some people's blood pumping but all I could see was a lot of old tables and chairs. I'm grateful to happen upon some type of weaponry exhibit, which is a little more exciting – there are swords, crossbows and guns aplenty but the novelty soon wears off as they're all behind glass and, despite pleading with one of the attendants, I'm not allowed to try any of them out.

I wander out into the rain and wind again to see if the views are up to much and am only saved from being blown off the castle walls by sheltering behind an enormous (fat) German man. I'm eternally grateful to him and give him a nod towards his belly and a double 'thumbs up' to indicate my thanks.

On returning to the hostel, everyone inside is hammered. It turns out that the rest of the hostel found out about the bank holiday and coupled with the horrible weather decided to spend the day getting plastered on Slovak beer – I'm notified that I'm playing major catch up and spend the next couple of hours fruitlessly attempting to get to the level of those around me. The group staggers into the city and manages to find a bar that's open, in the end I give up trying to find anyone who isn't leaning on something to stop themselves falling over (or falling asleep standing up – I've never got my head round that one), and make the decision to hit the hay and catch the early train to the Slovakian Tatras (it's a mountain range) the following morning to get some exercise and detox for a few days.

The Slovakian Tatras

I'm awoken at four in the morning by my drunken roommates returning from their night out and falling all over the place. One gives up trying to make the journey up to his top bunk and settles for the floor, another makes it as far as the bathroom but doesn't make it out again. I suddenly decide that there's no time like the present to get going and jump out of bed to set off right away for the Tatras. Day is breaking outside and commuters are on their way to work, a few quite rightly look at Clive and me and wonder what I'm doing up at such an ungodly hour of the morning – I'm beginning to wonder myself.

I find that I have become helplessly addicted to first-class tickets and purchase another one for the train to the 'low Tatras' (there are high and low Tatras – it's fairly simple to figure out why). This is going to become expensive if I can't shake the habit by the time I get to Western Europe. I wait on the platform and a man stares hard at me, unblinking. He's freaking me out more than a little so I make my way past him to the other end of the platform; his head revolves 360 degrees, following me all the while - a little unnerving. It transpires that this man/robot/alien works in the dining car, as later he serves me a sandwich and a coffee (without doing his revolving head trick) and says something to me in a language I don't understand (I'm almost certain it was something about him being a robot from the future who had been sent to kill me).

Four hours after leaving a dry and overcast Bratislava I arrive at the small town of Liptovsky Mikulas in the low Tatras. It's absolutely lashing it down with rain and after hurriedly (as hurriedly as you can in torrential rain carrying a heavy backpack) following the signs to the town centre I'm completely soaked through and freezing. All my warm clothes (1 x jeans, 1 x jumper) are drenched and I trudge into the tourist information office a broken (and wet and cold) man. The lady in the tourist information is amazingly helpful, she advises me on what to do (buy some warm clothing and waterproofs), where to go (somewhere inside), and finds me a little guesthouse a stone's throw away (I know this because I threw a stone from the tourist info and it smashed one of the guesthouse windows).

The guesthouse is an absolute classic. For the bargain sum of seven pounds (or whatever that is in Slovakian thingamajigs) I find myself standing in seventies heaven. I'm surrounded by chocolate brown, orange and lime green furnishings in a tiny twin room that is barely large enough for one person. There are even orange doilies on the bedside table. The shower room has a bewitching pastel blue theme and a surprisingly decent shower, apart from the miniscule curtain that only covers half of the cubicle, resulting in minor flooding of the room. Worryingly, there is also a padded door; I've got no idea of the significance of this.

On my way back down to the reception area I discover that there is a black door ajar on the main stairway and peer curiously through the gap, I see a reception desk manned by an attractive woman dressed in black. A couple of sheepish looking men brush pass me, entering the room and this leads me to the only assumption possible - that it's some kind of dodgy massage parlour. I consider entering and asking for 'the works' for research purposes but as I'm not entirely sure of the exact specialty of the establishment I decide against it. For now.

Where to go with no warm clothes when it's pouring with rain

The next poser was: where do you go with no warm clothes whilst it's pouring with rain – the answer? To an ice cave of course! I dig out my ski hat, don a dry pair of shorts and my sopping wet rain jacket (which instantly clings to my dry skin) and take a bus out to the cave. I'm distressed to find on arrival that you have to wait outside until the current tour is finished inside. I'm freezing (yes, I realise I'm wearing shorts) and shelter from the continuing downpour under a refreshment kiosk roof for 45 minutes, treating myself to a cup of hot mud and admiring the non-view of the low Tatras which I can't see for clouds and rain.

After my miserable wait I finally enter the ice cave and the guide, spotting my camera, asks if I've paid for a ticket. I show him my ticket but he explains that I require an extra ticket for my camera and after refusing my excuse of 'not buying one because I've got hypothermia and the coffee's shit' he pockets the cash I give him just to get the damn tour going. At first I'm pretty unimpressed as we take the steps downward into the cave, it's just bloody cold and dark but as we negotiate further there are some spectacular natural ice sculptures hanging from the roof of the cave, it's like a magical ice palace with wooden walkways and full of freezing tourists. I make the most of my legal camera status and snap off plenty of photos, mostly as evidence of how blue my skin was. On exiting the cave, it's stopped raining and I get my first clear glimpse of the low Tatras, this place reminds me of New Zealand. Or 'Middle Earth' as I believe it's now known.

I return to Liptovsky Mikulas and have a wander around the place now it's dried out, the compact town centre is pleasant enough without much to see but the outskirts seem a little on the dodgy side. My opinion on this may have been swayed by being constantly chased by angry dogs as I explored. The very edge of town offers some nice views of the surrounding countryside and the low tatras but the dark clouds were quickly gathering again so I rapidly made for the safety of my time warp hotel room.

The evening comes around and I visit a petite wooden traditional Slovakian restaurant – I have little idea what anything on the menu is (apart from Pivo of course – I try to translate 'beer' into the local dialect as soon as I possibly can) so decide to take a 'Golden Gastronomic Gamble' by pointing at the first thing on the menu that catches my eye. I end up being served Bratwurst, Sauerkraut and boiled potatoes, which does very nicely. I fail miserably trying to ask the young waitress for a dessert using hand and face signals and only succeed in making her piss herself laughing. I just point to something on the menu and hope – it turns out to be a fine apple strudel, which I'm overwhelmed with. I move on to a nearby pub and begin to work my way through the local beers; at bargain prices like these you can afford a couple of attempts at each to form an accurate critique. After (quite) a few beers and some unsuccessful attempts at making conversation with the locals (they look like they're going to kill me) I realise that the place is a tad rough and unwelcoming and head home.

There are some drunken kids causing trouble outside my hotel when I reach the front door – I explain to the group that I've paid seven pounds for this place and would appreciate some peace and quiet in return, they briefly take on board what I've got to say and continue fighting. It transpires that the padding on my room door is soundproofing and you can't hear a sound through it – a fantastic idea. Unfortunately all the walls are made of paper, which means you can hear everything from the adjoining rooms – I'm next to a chap with an incessant cough and a bladder problem that requires an hourly visit to the toilet. A real bonus.

Drinking Water

I've got some important advice for you here. When buying bottled drinking water abroad it's important to find out what the local words for 'gas' and 'no gas' are. Many times I think I've finally got this system perfected until after purchase when I hear a soul-destroying fizz on twisting my bottle cap. If no one's around, just take a leaf out of my book and turn the cap on a few different bottles until you find one that doesn't hiss.

The very best of luck to you.

Feeling a long way from home

Early evening back in Liptovsky Mikulas, I'm sitting in an Internet café and am shocked to see the news that London was bombed this morning. I'm absolutely zombified and look around to see if anyone else is talking about it but the place is full of noisy local kids playing online games. I'm becoming stressed and need a drink to calm me down, there's no one English in town to talk to or even anyone that speaks English, which is making me feel pretty lonely. The strange thing is, as I sat there drinking alone in a restaurant on the square I realised I was glad to have the isolation when hiking out in the Tatra's only hours before but am now in need of some company. I've a nasty feeling in the pit of my stomach and decide to write the night off so walk out to the local supermarket and buy a ridiculously cheap bottle of vodka (which tastes like lighter fluid – perhaps it was) and drink myself to sleep.

I'm awoken at 6am by the sound of bells and am beginning to wonder if I'd stolen an enormous church bell during the night, worn it as a hat before falling asleep and now someone was attacking me with an iron bar. It transpires that the din is coming from a church not too far away. This din is a stroke of luck as in my boozy state I'd forgotten to set my alarm clock. I hastily throw everything into Clive and check out, slightly upset about leaving my seventies wonderland. It's a beautiful, warm sunny day and a shame to have to leave the mountains. I'm still half drunk and on arrival at the train station think nothing of wandering across the tracks to a strip of concrete that serves as a platform to wait for my train. A guard shouts over and reprimands me in two languages (Slovak & German I think) for being out on the tracks before a train has arrived. I apologise profusely and retire to a nearby bench for a nap.

My transport arrives and I reluctantly take my seat next to a gargantuan, moustached woman sporting a crew cut. As the train speeds away from the picturesque mountains, hills, forests and rivers of the Tatras, back to Bratislava and on to Hungary, my last memory before I drift into sleep is the smell of 'Jabba the Hutt' next to me filling my nostrils with her foul bottom stench.

7 – Hungary

Bathing in Budapest

After spending a couple of hot, muggy days wandering aimlessly around Budapest, taking in the sights, I decide it's an opportune time to visit the city's famous baths. I ride the metro out to 'Szechenyi Furdo', finding myself in front of a large, grand, yellow building adorned with pillars and statues. I bungle my way through the slightly complex (for me) pricing structure at the ticket office (wherein you pay a sum of money on entering and then receive a refund on departing, based on the length of your stay), have a bit of trouble with the doorman (I think I was holding my ticket the wrong way up) and after some time wandering the wood clad corridors, make my way straight down into the midst of the communal women's changing rooms. Oh dear.

I grimace as I'm faced with the sight of several old women in the altogether and after an awkward smile and a wave, I sprint as fast as I can up the first stairway I find which leads me into the outdoor pool area, fully clothed and panting. I realise everyone is staring at me, give them a knowing nod and enlist the help of an attendant to guide me to the male changing room. It's here that I come face to face with what alarmingly appears at first to be a grizzly bear, but turns out to be a very hairy, naked man. Once I pull myself together, I change into my swimming costume and am given a locker by a surly chap dressed in tennis kit.

I make my way to the outdoor thermal baths and survey the scene. There's a pool for lane swimming (no swimming cap – no entry) and one for lounging around in. There are old Hungarian men playing chess in the baths, and I curse myself for not bringing my monopoly down. The surrounding buildings (all yellow) are filled with various temperature pools and saunas.

After bumping into some friends, we foolishly begin our tour of the bath's internal buildings with the world's hottest sauna (in my uneducated opinion) and it's absolutely unbearable. I'm pretty sure we've strolled into an oven by mistake and after less than a minute dramatically stagger out, gasping for air and plunge into a nearby cold pool – there's nothing like being roasted alive and then falling into a pool of ice I can tell you. There's a room that helps your breathing (eucalyptus I believe), the majority of this room was filled by one enormous fellow in extremely tight Speedos standing proudly in the centre with his hands on his hips and letting himself hang loose in all his glory. Beginning to feel a little nauseous, I averted my gaze only to (accidentally) plant it on the nether regions of a woman with terribly unkempt pubic hair – it looked like she was concealing an actual beaver beneath her swimsuit. Ugh.

I leave to sample the different temperature bathing pools, I'm always suspicious in those warm, cloudy ones that someone may have become ultimately relaxed and relieved themselves, subsequently I can never stay long in them, no matter what their healing properties are alleged to be (does a collection of various peoples urine heal anything?). The baths are busy and all the pools are fairly full; I find one with a space but when the couple next to me begins kissing, followed by some foreplay and move onto what looked like full intercourse, I realise that there are no signs outlawing 'heavy petting' here and bail out immediately. I continue on to a spinning whirlpool, whose ultra strong current sucks you in as you walk past minding your own business, resulting in you and whoever is unfortunate enough to be in the vicinity at the time being tumbled like laundry in a washing machine, with no escape until the program ends some minutes later – fun and incredibly strange. Once I make it out, I'm starting to turn into a prune so call time and collect my refund. Now that's relaxation.

House Party?

Following some re-hydration and a change of clothes I arrive at an al-fresco bar that looks to me like it was once (or perhaps still is) a metro station, I'm unable to confirm whether this is true or not, as the barmaid I asked thought I was more than a little strange. It's a pleasantly warm evening and the long, wide steps that lead down into the bar are packed with people sitting enjoying themselves. A small group of locals with musical instruments congregate at one side of the steps and, as I take a table with a few friends, I keep an eye on what they're up to. As I feared, they strike up a din involving several poorly tuned guitars, some bongos and a dimwit playing his beer glass, accompanied by some hideously out of tune singing. There seems to be no sign of the noise abating so we head to a bar/club in the middle of nowhere that appears to be someone's house.

A huge, grumpy, bearded doorman perches menacingly on a stool by the door, in front of a thick grey curtain that hides the buildings interior. Despite the uncertainty of what exactly this establishment may hold in store, our curiosity gets the better of us. We decide to go for it and all bundle into a graffiti covered dive. After a couple of beers in a courtyard filled with drunken students, an inebriated chap springs up on a table to make an important announcement - possibly that the table beneath him was about to collapse - which it duly did. After wiping away the tears of laughter we move upstairs to the 'dance floor' which is a darkened room with a few cheap disco lights and a couple of lads in the corner playing CD's on their home 'hi-fi' system. Extremely cheap beer was being served in plastic glasses from the kitchen nearby so, after discovering that there was a light switch by the 'stage' and hilariously flicking that on and off for a couple of minutes, we decide to get plastered, revel in the atmosphere and enjoy the night. The only other incident of note (apart from standing around having a chat on the dance floor whilst waiting for the CD's to be changed over) was that the upstairs bathroom was actually someone's bathroom, complete with bath, toiletries and bathroom cabinet. It was next door to a small kitchenette, which made me realise that this really was someone's house – I wonder if they knew what was going on?

Train to Lake Balaton

I take a train over to Lake Balaton the next morning; it's the largest lake in Central Europe - 77km long. I'm unsure whether I'm boarding the right train and ask a few locals who don't speak English but nod when I ask 'Balaton?' and that's more than good enough for me to make a decision. The rain starts shortly after we set off and the windows become clouded with condensation. I have no information on my destination other than the name of the station I want (Revfulop) and each time the train halts I furiously wipe the steamy window and try to find some identification on the station. A kind Hungarian man who has noticed my blind panic every time the train stops (hey, we could be heading anywhere) sits beside me and shows me that he has a book with the timetables in it. He speaks no English but we manage to communicate by writing on the misty window (this is exciting new ground in my communication skills) and identify that I am on the correct train but my stop is still some way away so I can relax. A child sitting across the aisle pukes an impressive amount of vomit (I'd say a good litre) onto the floor and is carted off to the toilet by his mother, leaving us with a nice smelly carriage. The train begins to stop at regular intervals in the middle of nowhere with seemingly no one embarking or disembarking and then finally gives up altogether at a level crossing where it sits motionless, blocking the road for 45 minutes. People begin climbing off and those stuck at the level crossing have left their stationary cars and are gesturing at the train, wondering what on earth is going on. There's a lot of conversation flying around the carriage and I'm included in this but obviously don't have any idea what they're discussing – I just raise my eyebrows, shake my head and 'tut' which seems to do the trick.

I finally arrive at good old Revfulop and bid farewell to my friends in the carriage (I wave – I've forgotten the Hungarian for goodbye). I set out toward the hostel I've booked and see a man walking towards me smiling and waving; it turns out that he's come to meet me off the train – what a lovely man. I'm shown around the wood cabin hostel (which has a bar but no kitchen) and am given a four bed dorm room all to myself. Having sat on a train for the majority of the day I'm keen for some fresh air and exercise and so take a walk up to the top of the town's hill where there sits a strange looking brick and wood, yellow lookout tower – it reminds me of a helter skelter but without the slide – perhaps that's a thought for future development. It's guarded by an old boy who sits in a little office underneath and collects money for climbing the tower (possibly toward the development of the aforementioned slide). Gladly it's not too high so there aren't hundreds of stairs to negotiate and once at the top you see a fine panoramic view over the town and the massive great lake it sits beside.

After working up a fair sweat with the hill climbing I head down to the lake's shore where I take a swim to cool down. Some fairly evil-looking swans start to head towards me in what appears to be an attack formation. Carnage looks imminent so I hastily retreat to the shore and relax with a book. That is until the sky clouds over, and thousands of mosquitoes arrive and launch a mass offensive on my person. I hurriedly dress whilst running back to the hostel shrieking, attracting some pointing and laughing from Hungarian tourists.

A rainy day with the locals

I'd arranged a countryside bike tour with one of the Hungarian lads working at the hostel but on awakening the next day it was pissing down rain again so I had to cancel. My happy host senses my downbeat mood and begins to organise other possibilities for my day: he tells me of a natural thermal bath with healing properties and, as I'd slightly tweaked a groin on my walk the previous day (and aggravated it scarpering from the mosquitoes), it sounds like a decent idea. In a nutshell, what followed was a rather tedious bus trip to sit in a warm lake in the rain.

The rain has worsened when I return to Revfulop and I hurry back to the hostel to avoid a serious drenching. It's three in the afternoon and the local drunk has just cracked open a bottle of Hungarian red at the bar and enthusiastically beckons me to join him.

So, it came to pass that the remainder of my time in Hungary was spent sheltering from the rain with a crowd of locals, getting totaled on wine and frequent shots of strong Hungarian liquor. I hadn't the faintest clue what any of my new friends were saying (may have been: 'I hope this English tosser is going to chip in for all this booze we're getting through') but had an enjoyable afternoon attempting to learn some Hungarian and teach 'British English' (as was requested of me). I manage to attract the affections of a cute (yet worryingly clingy) Hungarian lass who I spend the night wearing as an apron/koala bear. She simply will not let go of me and pleads with me to stay in Balaton and take her for romantic bike rides instead of leaving the next day. As her tipsy, not unwelcome affection begins to sway toward brazen, drunken obsession I manage to cleverly ditch her by offering her my turn in a darts game as a sign of my undying love and running away as fast as my legs could carry me.

8 – Croatia

Hvar

I'd travelled from Balaton into Croatia, pausing briefly in Zagreb before heading south and stopping for a night in Split, Dalmatia, hatching a plan to try and meet 101 locals in the region to make for a hilarious anecdote. Unfortunately, I don't meet nearly enough people and '43 Dalmatians' doesn't have quite the same ring to it so I abandon the idea. Even early the following morning, it's fast becoming a baking hot day and the heat during the walk to the harbour, combined with Clive's weight proves for a real physical struggle. I reach my goal, purchase a ticket to the island of Hvar and make for my designated catamaran.

I have the pleasure of sitting next to a stunning blonde woman on the catamaran and, after striking up a conversation, discover that she is an investment banker, born on Hvar, living and working in Zurich and returning home to visit her parents. She explains that the most beautiful women in Europe are to be found on Hvar and I'm not in any position to disagree with her. After an hour we approach the island and she points out her parent's house: it looks pretty grand, and I await my dinner invite for this evening but it doesn't arrive. I think the fact that I haven't showered for a couple of days may have something to do with it. You don't see many backpacker and investment banker couples around.

I'm getting lucky with the hostels in Croatia. They are few and far between, but I've managed to find a bed on every stop of the way so far. The only hostel on the island has one bed left for the night - although they're full the following night, I'm advised to arrange some accommodation with the 'grannies' – the lack of budget accommodation in Croatia means that these ladies can make some extra money by renting out their spare rooms to backpackers. They wait for boats to come in, hold pictures of their rooms (or ones they've cut out of a home style magazine) on hand-made signs and then scramble for business when the punters arrive on shore. So, in this instance, I'm able to scoot past the throng of grannies gathering in the sunshine and meet a representative from the hostel who is due to meet me off the boat. They don't arrive though, and after a quick phone call I'm told that I need to make my own way to the house (it's up on a hill of course) and arrive some time later a tired, sweaty mess. I begin to wonder if I can do an equipment review and shed some of Clive's weight to make these summer hikes a little easier.

A 'popular' beach

My first full day on Hvar is another scorcher, I've no idea how hot it is but rest assured it's around the 'bloody hot' mark. I take a wander down to the harbour and have a look at the flock of small boats that are setting out to the neighbouring islands this morning, each has a keen boat owner holding a sign displaying an island name touting for business and ushering tourists on board. I haven't really looked into which island is a winner, so just take a gamble and jump onto a boat that seems popular. We motor away into the open water, leaving Hvar behind and dock at 'wherever it is'. I'm slightly taken aback to be confronted immediately with full-frontal male nudity as I climb off the boat and reach the end of the concrete pier that meets the rocky beach. I brush past the old bearded man with his wares proudly on display for the newcomers and hastily make for some nearby woods to decide on a contingency plan. I discover another beach at the rear of the island and it's the same situation here – genitalia everywhere.

Realising I'm stuck here on 'stark naked island' until the next boat arrives in a couple of hours, I hire a sun bed and try to find a rock with some breathing space from the gallivanting naked pensioners festival. I briefly consider joining in but realise that the only people walking around in the altogether are the older generation. Everyone under the age of fifty seems to be wearing something (other than a grin). The nearest chap down from me sits naked astride a sun bed, vigorously oiling his genitals and I decide a swim is in order to get away from this madness. I awkwardly clamber barefooted across the jagged rocks toward the seafront, trying not to stumble into any of the mounds of flesh positioned around me, I almost clatter into a ghostly pale woman whose breasts are down to her waist and finally reach the seafront only for my entrance to be blocked by a grinning fellow proudly standing 'au natural' with his hands on his hips, almost thrusting toward me. In blind panic I barge him, briefly glimpsing the unwelcome sight of his pubic moustache crawling down his legs as I fall into the water close to vomiting. I hide in the water for as long as humanely possible, getting frazzled by the sun in the process and make a run for it once the boat returns. I've seen more naked pensioners in the last week than I need to in a lifetime.

'When I needed a Shelter'

I'm on a ferry from the islands down to Dubrovnik and, as we dock, I've already hatched a plan, I know there's only one hostel in town and I'm pretty confident of getting a bed there following my luck so far. The ferry door lowers onto the harbour and I dash ahead of the couples and groups who are discussing their next move, past a vocal group of grannies waving signs and arrive at the hostel half an hour later, well in front of the chasing pack. The hostel is absolutely full for the next three days so my luck has come to an end. As I contemplate a twenty-minute walk toward the old town with Clive on my shoulders in thirty degree heat, I hear a voice nearby - an old gentleman has noticed my quandary and kindly offers me a room in his house - on the proviso that I have a friend who can take the other bed. I inform him that sadly I haven't got any friends and ask whether it would be possible for me to take the room on my own. He's not having any of it and suggests I go and make a friend and return. I reluctantly trek to the old town to see if the tourist office can help me find somewhere cheap, or a friend.

I make it into Dubrovnik's old town and can just about make out what a stunning place it is through the sea of sweat that's stinging my eyes - a walled fortress filled with some spectacular architecture, white paved pedestrian streets, narrow alleyways, stairways that seem to go up forever and bucket loads of tourists. I call in at tourist information but the price of a single room is far more than I can afford, so I ask them what budget options are available to me and they suggest finding a granny and give me a couple of locations around the old town where they are known to gather to tout business. After spending another hour walking around in the stifling heat, dragging Clive and soaked through with sweat, there are no grannies to be seen. As I begin to lose all hope and start to plan a night on the streets, a large woman, wearing a bright yellow tent and sporting a bushy moustache, approaches me:

She: "You looking for room boy?"

Me: "What do you have?"

She: "I have no room."

Me: "Thank you. That's incredibly helpful."

She: "But the sisters, they may have room"

Me: "The sisters eh? And where would I find your sisters?"

The woman nods and points me to a nearby door where I would find (I imagine) two more ugly (that's an additional two, not two 'more ugly' – there couldn't possibly be an uglier woman) sisters and a younger beautiful sister performing household chores and wanting to go to the ball. I ring the bell as directed and the door opens, I step into a dark, empty room and try to adjust my sight to the poor light.

All of a sudden an old woman dressed as a nun appears out of nowhere. Now either: a) I'd just walked into one sick party or b) I was about to try and spend the night in a nunnery. When, after a couple of minutes, several smiling nuns surround me (ah! I get it! The sisters!) Speaking in Italian and stroking my hair, I must admit I was leaning towards the former but it transpires that the latter was true. They name their price, and not knowing whether I'm permitted to haggle with women of the cloth, I instantly agree. They say something in Italian that at the time I believed was 'Do you choose to repent evil and all your sins?' but with hindsight may well have been 'try not to leave pubic hairs in the shower tray love'. A nun then directed me (wearing what I imagined is the away strip - white getup with black headband) to my 'chamber' and there it was - complete with writing desk (with crucifix above) and a picture of the Virgin Mary hanging above my bed. And that, my brothers and sisters, is how I was rescued by our Lord on the streets of Dubrovnik.

9 – Slovenia

It's an enjoyable and picturesque train ride from Zagreb to Ljubljana, speeding past greenery, trees, hills, rivers, little farms and houses. The police undertaking the passport control at the border begin searching through the bag of the guy sitting opposite me, one of them stares me in the eye intensely and asks if I have anything to declare. I begin to feel almost as guilty as you do walking through the green channel at customs on return from a summer holiday even though I've got absolutely nothing dodgy on me. I wonder if I should declare my pasta but decide not to bother. They shoot the man opposite and leave.

Hill climbing

To be honest, I've been feeling a little guilty since witnessing an American fellow's 'dorm workout' (he did some push ups, sit ups and some kind of arm strengthening exercise using a chair) the previous evening and realise that all this drinking and sitting on public transport is not doing much for my physical well-being. I vow to make an effort to stay in relatively decent shape and go to the tourist office to see if they have any suggestions for an energetic excursion this afternoon – they tell me of a mountain known as 'Smarna Gora' and I accept the mission.

I arrive at the foot of the mountain (maybe it's just a big hill, it's only 670m high), look uphill through the trees and begin to work through my psyche-up routine. As I'm about to put my best foot forward, a woman dressed in red, sporting leggings and a headband comes steaming out of the woodland in some kind of frenzied power walk, pumping a set of ski poles, and I'm left in a spin as she brushes past me and disappears. I compose myself and set off but only moments later, a Slovenian hill walking champion zooms past me. I see this as a challenge to my ability and quickly pursue the wiry fellow up the dirt slope, tripping over an unseen tree root and landing on my face. An old guy strides past shaking his head at my amateurish incompetence. I pledge to improve and with an increased level of concentration march upward, keeping a keen eye out for obstacles. Further up, I'm in full flow and proudly nod at a woman on her way down who returns my compliment, another two athletes pass and nod – acceptance at last! No one else passes me and I'm on fire as I reach the summit of the mountain, stopping only briefly at a bell which is alleged to prevent toothache if you pull the rope with your teeth, I do just that and am overjoyed at not only being a hill-walking champion but also saving a fortune on dental fees.

At Smarna Gora's summit there's a church and a snack shop - I forgo the church visit, grab a drink and have a look over the lush countryside from way up high whilst catching my breath. I think I can see Ljubljana in the distance but it's a little cloudy so I can't be sure. I return to the bottom of the mountain as a champion, exchanging knowing nods with fellow hill walkers on my way down. The driver of my bus back to Ljubljana is having a cigarette break, leaning against his empty bus. He takes a photo of the mountain and me and explains that he once climbed it; we sit and swap glory stories, reminiscing about the good old days. An old lady walking her dog gasps at the mountain, points at me and stares in awe – 'Yes love. I nailed it'.

10 – Italy

Venice

My train arrives in Venice, which marks a third of the way through the trip – almost certainly the easiest third. Walking down the train station steps and being enveloped by the busy city, I'm greeted by stifling heat, hordes of tourists and canals instead of roads (I knew about this one and don't understand the big deal – when the housing estate, cinema and pub down the road from me flooded a few years ago there wasn't a tourist to be seen). A sea of cigarette butts litters the pathways and a bevy of African men sell fake sunglasses and handbags from makeshift cardboard stalls on the pavements.

Now, I knew that the next few weeks in Western Europe were going to be a major test of my budget and had accounted for this, and so need to take a step downward in the accommodation stakes and be content with camping. Not that I mind that of course: I've always enjoyed camping at home but must admit that I've never experienced sharing a tent with a stranger (unless it's someone breaking into my tent whilst I'm asleep at a festival), which is what I'm scheduled to do once I locate my campsite in Venice.

I take a bus a short while out of Venice and find the campsite, make my way to my little green 'house tent' (meaning that the camp site own the tents, not that it's the size of a house – quite the opposite), claim one of the two beds on offer and lock the door/tent flap before investigating what the campsite has to offer me. It seems that we're camping on an airstrip, as planes are taking off and landing near the bar area. Whilst I'm figuring out what impact this will have on my night's sleep, I make the decision that it's far too hot to go sightseeing and spend the rest of the afternoon sitting by the campsite swimming pool enjoying the weather and getting acquainted with the local beer.

Not liking Pigeons

My 'getting acquainted with the local beer' initiative the night previous means that I'm a real sorry, hung-over mess as I head back into Venice and, before I know it, I've spent two brainless hours wandering aimlessly around the city without a map. I've absolutely no idea where I am so decide to go back to the beginning and start over again – this time engaging my brain. On the way I notice a stall selling shitty comedy t-shirts like one was able to buy from reputable market stalls in the eighties ('adihash' for example) – I search for a 'loadsamoney' one but there's no sign. The vendor doesn't seem to be very busy (which isn't surprising considering the quality of his merchandise) so I consider suggesting that he could sweep up a few of these cigarette butts, but he's not the happiest looking soul in the world so I decide against it.

I manage to purchase a map at a ticket office for the river ferries and finally get my day on course by boarding a water taxi to Piazza San Marco - probably the most popular tourist destination in Venice. The main draw for the thousands of tourists is San Marco's Basilica – a huge cathedral adorned with gold mosaics and statues. As churches go it's a spectacular sight. Also on the Piazza is the huge Bell Tower, which you can climb for views over the square. I seem to have discovered the square at the peak time of the day, as all the queues were ridiculously long, and queuing to see the inside of a church (no matter how impressive it may be) for an hour in this oppressive heat with a hangover doesn't appeal to me at all. As wonderful as the architecture around the Piazza is, there is one feature that spoils it somewhat (other than the fact that you're sharing it with thousands of tourists) – the bloody pigeons.

I absolutely despise pigeons. There's no other way to put it. Don't get me wrong, I'm not scared of them and haven't had any childhood experiences that could have developed a pigeon phobia (what would that be called?) but their uselessness, coupled with their popularity absolutely baffles me. Here in Piazza San Marco people actually pay a euro to buy bread to give to the vermin! I'm not trying to ruin people's holidays here and am more than happy for young children to continue gleefully chasing them around the square, but draw the line at adults rejoicing in being covered in the filthy buggers. I mean, Can you imagine queuing up at your local kebab house and paying a man outside to feed the rats down the back alley? You can? Oh, alright then. Anyway, the pigeons almost outnumber the tourists and that's an awful lot of pigeons. I pause for a rest on a step (the café's on the square would cost me a weeks budget for a cappuccino) and am happy taking in the views and doing a spot of people watching but soon grow tired of constantly kicking out at the stupid pigeons that scuttle near me, mistaking cigarette ends for crumbs. The thick bastards.

Florence - Seeing 'Dave'

I arrive in a humid Florence in the midst of sunset and attempt to locate my bus to the campsite. I spend some time trying to track down the 'number 12' I'd been advised to catch in my email from the campsite. I ask the fellow at the ticket office and am informed that 'twelve is now thirteen'. This creates all kinds of scenarios in my head (is twelve now unlucky for some?) but I run with it and - lo and behold! - arrive at my campsite right at the top of a hill and slap bang next to Piazza Michelangelo: a square located on the opposite side of the river Arno, facing the city and offering magnificent views over all of Florence – not a bad location at all!

The morning heat fills my tiny tent and I emerge to hazy sunshine. I make my way down the hill, buying breakfast from a small family store along the way, across the river Arno on the Ponte Vecchio (a bridge with lots of shops selling expensive gold and silver jewelry) and into the city. I pass the Galleria Uffuzi, which is already attracting a huge queue. I can only afford to visit one gallery here and have already decided that I want to see 'David' at the Galleria Dell'Accademia. For a reason unbeknown to me, I make a strange decision not to pass by there until the hottest part of the day when the sun is blazing high above the city and there's little shade to hide in. There's some sort of protest going on at the sprawling Piazza Della Signoria but I can't make out what it's for, so I mingle amongst the banners and whistle blowers and shout a few Italian pasta dishes which draw me some funny looks and I decide to remove myself from the protest. Piazza Della Signoria is home to many statues, fountains, ice cream shops and the imposing Palazzo Vecchio, a castle like block of a building with a tower extending from its top. It's a hive of activity and a good place to take the weight off your feet, get some water on board, treat yourself to a gelato and do some good old people watching.

I reach the awesome Duomo. Apparently it's the fourth largest cathedral in the world and, believe me when I tell you, it's absolutely bloody massive. It is an enormous white, pink and green building with a huge dome and bell tower beside it. Once again the crowds had amassed to view the inside and climb the tower and I had to be content with a couple of laps around it, admiring the architecture on the walls and doors. Time was running out and I still had to queue to see David (or Dave as I saw fit to call him). I just have enough time to walk the markets at San Lorenzo where a group of African men are hastily de-assembling their 'easy to pack up if you're in a bit of a rush' cardboard pitches as a couple of policemen are spotted.

I arrive at the Galleria Dell'Accademia tired and hungry. The queue to get inside stretches forever so I buy some bread and cheese from a nearby shop and take a seat at a small piazza nearby. All the seats in the minimal shade are taken, apart from one next to an old, bald fellow dressed in jeans and a short sleeved blue shirt, muttering to himself and lighting one cigarette after another, taking a single drag and then throwing them to the floor. I decide I'll risk the sun and take a bench nearby. The old guy begins to hurl abuse (I think) at me and I look down and mind my own business until his shouting subsides. He's joined by a woman who laughs every time he throws one of his cigarettes down, and I can't help but chuckle as the same thing happens over and over again: he lights a cigarette, takes a drag and throws it and she bursts into hysterical laughter, which halts as soon as he puts the next cigarette into his mouth. I wonder how many cigarettes this guy goes through in one day, how much money he spends and whether his female friend and he live out this same scene every day, before growing bored of the repetitive entertainment and walking back to join the queue at the Galleria.

It's unbelievably hot and the piles of empty water bottles by the overflowing bins are testament to that. I take my battered flip-flops off to inspect my feet: they're blistering up quite nicely. I know I should have worn shoes but they just don't go well with shorts – I can't afford a fashion faux pas of that magnitude in Italy. Wherever there is a minute chance of some shade the queue snakes toward it. I'm behind a group of rich, loud middle-aged American couples and resort to humming to myself to try and drown out their shrill voices. After an hour and a half I finally reach the front of the queue, pay my one and only entrance fee of the day and enter the Galleria. As everyone is rushing straight to see David I take a look around the gallery at the other paintings and sculptures on display before curiosity gets the better of me and I head to the main attraction. I'm surprised to find that I'm quite taken aback when I see him, having seen many pictures of the sculpture (plus the copy at the Piazza Michelangelo); I wasn't expecting to be so impressed by the real McCoy. The first thing that strikes me is the sheer size of the dude; he's an absolute beast of a man! That whole David & Goliath story is a load of balderdash. David must be at least 15 feet tall and he's remarkably well built for a child. Even with just a slingshot he could do some serious damage, I'd have had him down as the favourite. Michelangelo made the sculpture from a single block of marble and there's just an aura about it when you walk around – I'm glad I made the effort to come and see it.

I wait wearily for a bus back up to the campsite, caked in sweat, my aching legs are covered with grime and I don't smell too sweet. I stand in anticipation for twenty minutes but there are no buses forthcoming and it takes all my remaining willpower and energy to walk uphill, across Piazza Michelangelo and to the campsite. Walking back to my tent, I pass the fenced area housing the bins and almost vomit - have you ever smelt bins when it's the late thirties? (The temperature I mean, not the era, why would any of you have smelt bins in the 1930's? Unless you had a time machine of course...). I slump at one of the picnic benches with an ice-cold beer; it tastes phenomenal and lasts less than a minute. I don't get up for a very long time.

Creating havoc the Italian way

The queues at Florence train station are ridiculous and, on this occasion, I haven't arranged a ticket in advance. I've already missed one train to Rome whilst I'm queuing but there's a delayed one that's due to arrive shortly so I snap up a ticket for that. I've noticed something strange about the way they announce trains in Italy: the person operating the departures board will wait until a throng of sweaty, bemused, American and Japanese tourists and smelly, bored backpackers (including yours truly - hello) gather in increasing numbers facing the board. At the very last possible minute, and once there is a sufficient safety risk the platform number will be displayed, creating absolute mayhem and with any luck causing slight injury and a possible missing of the train.

I hover at the rear of said throng and, once the platform is announced, spring into action and move well clear of the chasing pack, board the train and locate my seat. An orange American lady with huge bingo wings (the bits of fatty skin that hang from your arms) is causing a fuss by sitting in someone else's seat. She argues that she wants to face the way the train is travelling and is trying to get her husband to back her up; he looks like he would really rather be somewhere else (and with someone else). There's a pretty Italian girl sitting across from me, dressed all in black (something expensive looking) and she's wearing the biggest pair of sunglasses I've ever seen, absolutely ridiculous they are, covering half her face – I wonder if she's wearing them for a joke but figure it's probably fashion. I resolve to buy myself a pair as soon as humanly possible.

Seeing Rome in a day

I'm up and out of my tent bright and early with a jam-packed day planned. The day doesn't begin well, there's a severe lack of loo roll in the men's toilet block. I've made an elementary error and forgotten to check the availability of toilet tissue before sitting down and 'commencing play'. Fortunately, as I'm beginning to panic and search my pockets for decent sized till receipts, a child in a nearby cubicle despairingly cries out to his mum in the adjoining ladies block and she brings some in. The sheer relief of those stranded in the cubicles wondering what to do next is clearly audible as we hold a cross-cubicle team meeting and agree a 'take some and pass it on' method between us to distribute the solitary toilet paper supply.

I'm keen to get my train tickets sorted for my onward journey the following night so my first port of call is the train station. I take my numbered ticket for service at the ticket office but there's quite some way until my turn, so I slope off to find some cheap breakfast before returning an hour later just in the nick of time. The ticket lady doesn't speak English but knows a little French and I'm able to communicate my needs using the broken French that I can remember from school. I'm horrified to find that the night trains for the next two nights are completely booked and the only train with available space in the next two days is first thing tomorrow. That leaves me with only one day to see all of Rome – now it's really on.

By the time I exit the metro at the Coliseum it's almost midday and when I see the structure for the first time the hairs stand up on the back of my neck - its sheer presence is overwhelming. As I'm looking up in admiration, some fellow dressed up in plastic gladiator gear comes over and asks me if I want to pay him for a photo. I point out that he's not going to last very long with plastic protective gear before challenging him to a fight to the death, which he refuses. As expected, I'm faced with more lengthy queues to enter and it takes some time to get inside. Once in the stadium I'm surprised to find that it's not in a fit state to host any event and the arena floor is non-existent, revealing the cells and areas where the animals were kept. Slightly disappointed that I'm not going to see a man in a skirt fight a tiger, I make do with walking the ruin, striding menacingly up the tunnels pretending to be about to fight for my honour (in reality I was trying to find the toilets) and hovering looking disinterestedly in the opposite direction close enough to assorted guided tours to listen in on the commentary because I couldn't afford to go on one – this is an art in itself.

I pass the striking Arch of Constantine and into the Roman Forum – the heart of ancient Rome. Once the political and social centre and now a sprawl of ruins that could tell hundreds of stories (it's a shame stone can't talk). I weave my way past the pushchairs getting stuck in between the bulky cobblestones and the tourists fainting from the heat or searching for shade and imagine what it would have been like nearly two thousand years ago. I'm gutted that I can't spend longer investigating but promise to come back and give Rome the time it deserves on a more relaxed trip. I visit Piazza Venezia and come face to face with the gargantuan Victor Emanuel monument, apparently the locals dislike this big, white building and know it as the 'wedding cake' or 'typewriter' – both seem pretty accurate to me.

I head towards the Pantheon and hastily grab some lunch (and a gelato) before ducking inside to have a look. The Pantheon is Rome's best preserved monument – it's in great nick, made as a temple to the gods and contains the tombs of kings, queens and Raphael (the renaissance painter rather than the teenage mutant ninja turtle) It also has a great big bloody hole in the dome roof to shed some light into the darkened building so you get wet if it rains.

I steam through the Piazza Colonna on my way to the magnificent Trevi Fountain - the most famous in Rome. It is dominated by statues of Neptune and his sea horses (amongst others) and a massive tourist draw. Adults and children alike waited for a spot on the edge to dip their feet in the cool water or throw a coin in as legend has it that if you put in a coin you shall return to Rome (bit of a crappy legend if you ask me - If you want to return you'll find a way regardless of whether you chuck a coin in a fountain). I'm running out of time, I find Piazza di Spagna and climb the Spanish steps and as the day draws to a close, stagger across the sweeping square of Piazza Del Popolo with its twin churches and giant obelisk. I summon my last drops of energy for the walk up to Pincio terrace and the amazing views over the city, trying to pinpoint the many landmarks I've spent the day trawling around in the cityscape.

It comes as a surprise to discover that I've already maxed my credit card at this early stage of the journey (must be the hefty charge that my bank makes every time I take out cash abroad – the greedy bastards). I'd visited a cash point to take out some spending money and the transaction was refused. This put me in the slightly surreal situation of standing in a busy piazza on a pay-phone to my bank to plead for some more money – the kind lady gives me another £600. Whilst I'm breathing a sigh of relief and marvelling at the moped mayhem on the streets I'm nearly taken out by some clown whilst on a zebra crossing (it's my fault for believing that someone would take notice of it) – I show my displeasure with a gesture that I think is an Italian insult (I believe I saw it on the Sopranos).

My evening is spent watching a mediocre pub singer performing a cabaret set at the campsite before retreating to my tent and being kept awake (along with the rest of the site) by a loud, drunken Scottish girl with a laugh like a choking goat on one side and a couple having loud sex (including some light spanking) on the other – the noise eventually dies down at 4am and I manage to grab a couple of hours sleep before having to rise for my train.

Roma to Genova

The Roma metro is strangely quiet for eight o clock on a Friday morning as I head to the train station, if this was the London underground then it would be absolute carnage – perhaps it's a holiday – who knows? I make it to the station in good time for once, board my train and, as the departure time passes by, everyone just sits in anticipation. Suddenly mayhem breaks out, everyone leaps to their feet, voices are raised and there are lots of hand gestures and exaggerated facial expressions. I'm feeling left out so stand and join in, muttering cult 1980's Italian footballers under my breath (Schillachi, Tardelli, Maldini, Baresi) and raising my eyebrows a lot. From what I can gauge, someone's bag has been lost. We all pour as a group out of the compartment and into the corridor towards the door, and even louder voices and more gestures follow. The train pulls away and, after a short, tense silence, a bag is hoisted aloft – we've got it! Cheers erupt, the group is overjoyed, and we all take our seats, thankful that everything has turned out alright. The trip to Genoa was wonderful: we spoke in Italian (they did), laughed, shared our food (theirs, I didn't think anyone would be interested in dry pasta), we passed rolling green hills, briefly glimpsed the sea and five hours later arrived in Genoa – We bid each other a warm farewell and I'm a little gutted that our merry gang is disbanded, even though I didn't understand a word that was spoken in five hours.

11 – France

Nice

I've decided to stop for a long weekend in the Cote d'Azur, having spent the entire day sitting on trains. I always try and book night trains for long journeys, as it's 'dead time', and you don't notice the hours slipping by so much (and it isn't as dull because you're hopefully sleeping) but when there's not a night service available (such as this occasion) you just have to bite the bullet and waste a day sitting and waiting to get somewhere. On arrival at Nice Gare, it's early evening and dark. I take a bus to Saint Maurice, which is up in the hills, out of town. I alight at the village square and am more than a little lost, but with a stroke of luck, the local hostel's shuttle bus is passing through on the way back from the train station and I manage to score a lift up the steep hill to the hostel. I'm bored and fatigued from the trains and just want a nice, cold beer but have to wait for the check-in and introductory talk before I'm presented with my key and a local map (always handy when you have no sense of direction). I make my way up to my dorm: it's light, airy, and, judging by the amount of packs on the floor, fully booked. I take the only available bunk (as luck would have it, it's a bottom bunk), leave Clive to get acclimatised and head down to the bar for a beer or two to celebrate my good 'bunk fortune'.

The makeshift bar (a table and a fridge) is housed in an old church. This seems slightly controversial but I'm more than happy to go along with it. I lounge around, converse with a few of my fellow residents and am taken aback to discover that my recent diet of beer, pizza and gelatos, coupled with exercise only when I'm feeling extremely guilty has resulted in me growing a healthy set of love handles/muffin tops/a fat back. I pledge to improve my diet whilst getting more exercise and order another beer whilst I try to formulate a plan.

Exploring Nice

It's a beautiful morning in Nice – hot and sunny with deep blue skies. I'm impressed with my French skills as I briefly manage to hold down a conversation with the bus driver but as soon as we move out of the 'Tricolore' textbook range, I'm completely stumped. I smile, shrug and sheepishly take my seat. I waste the first half of the day back at the train station, trying to sort out a ticket for the night train to Barcelona tonight. After a long wait for my ticket number to come round, I'm delighted to hear that they have space and book a couchette (sleeping compartment). As I make for the beach I discover that there seem to be absolutely no laws around dog care here. This results in dogs being allowed absolutely anywhere and copious amounts of dog shit. After dodging the intermittent piles of shit I eventually make it down to the brilliant blue seafront, chuckling as I pass the men occupying the benches along the boardwalk overlooking the beach, perving at the many topless female sunbathers. After a couple of hours comparing boobs with them, I decide to spend a short while relaxing on the stony beach. There's a constant stream of vendors passing by, offering soft drinks and beer whilst planes drop down to a few feet above our heads to land somewhere just behind us. A tramp strolls (falls) down the steps onto the beach, stands under one of the showers fully clothed until he's completely drenched and then buggers off in search of his mislaid begging cup, much to the amazement of all looking on - now that's what I call 'textbook tramping'. I consider going for a swim but don't want to look like an idiot tiptoeing barefoot across the pebbles so don't bother. Suddenly the police are on the beach, blowing whistles and pulling everyone out of the sea. I've no idea why this is happening so assume there's a killer shark on the loose.

Everything quiets down and, without any police or tramp showering, I get quite bored, so I head towards the old town, being wary of dog shit along the way – don't they have pooper scoopers in France? The old town is nice enough, with its side streets, cafes and bars (there was a market but I arrived too late and now there's just a clean up operation in progress). It's a little grittier than most I've visited and has a few too many beggars and hoboes for me to become enamoured with it. I'm more than happy with the Panini I bought from a little sandwich shop in an alley though – very tasty indeed, it was so darn good

I bought one for the train as well (the train journey I mean, I'm not making an offering of food for a train).

After my weekend in the Cote d'Azur comes to an end I manage to scrounge a lift to the train station and join the misfits and fellow backpackers leaning against the wall at the station front. I crack open one of the beers I'd purchased for the journey and notice a scared looking girl nearby (I'm not surprised, as the area around the station is notoriously dodgy at night – it's frequented by smelly, beer drinking backpackers), she's a South Korean student and I strike up a conversation to try and put her at ease. A beggar shows up and begins to work his way down the line of people; he obviously hasn't undertaken extensive market research, backpackers who are living off next to nothing themselves aren't an ideal demographic. He reaches me and requests a cigarette; I tell him that I don't smoke. He asks for a beer and I tell him I've only got the one I'm holding. He wants money (actually he asks for a minimum contribution of fifty cents) – I tell him to go away and he gets angry, kicks a wall and begins to scream at a couple walking past. I decide to move inside, safely away from the begging zone, head to the platform and await my train to Barcelona.

12 – Spain

To Granada

After spending a pleasant few days relaxing and sightseeing in Barcelona, I take a train to Granada. My train is an absolute beauty; real luxurious stuff: air conditioning, big comfy seats, ample leg room and even free headphones to watch movies (Spanish – obviously) and listen to music. The landscape becomes dryer and dustier as we near Granada, with yellow and browns dominating. We pull into the town in the early afternoon, I can tell it's going to be hot outside (people were melting) and briefly consider staying on the nice cool air-conditioned train and seeing where we end up. I'm slightly concerned that it may take me back to somewhere I've already been so disembark at the last moment, stepping into an absolute oven of a town; I was nicely roasted in just twelve minutes, and must have looked remarkably similar to a pig on the spit, as I was eating an apple at the time.

I locate my hostel and receive such a warm and friendly welcome that I instantly feel that I'm going to love it here, I'm informed that there is a trip out to some hot springs tonight and, being something of a connoisseur of baths by now, I'm happy to sign up for it. I spend the remainder of the afternoon in the Albaycin – Granada's old Arab quarter. The neighbourhood is spread over a hill and is awash with tourists. Small shops and tea houses fill the lower region of the narrow, cobbled streets and alleys (it reminds me of an Indiana Jones film) and as you walk upwards you can begin to see the whitewashed houses in all their glory, as well as a stirring view across to the magnificent 'Alhambra' – a monumental fortress filled with palaces and gardens, sitting amongst a mass of trees. I've been told that Campo Principe is a good place to find some decent food but arrive there a little early in the evening. The local restaurateurs are just arising from their siestas and setting up the tables and chairs outside their establishments. I sit in a nearby square and wait for them to open, slightly disappointed that I've missed a legitimate reason for an afternoon nap.

Kidnapped/Hot Springs

The evening comes and, after a couple of beers up on the hostels rooftop bar whilst admiring the city by night, a group from the hostel make for the fountain at Plaza de Isabel Catolica – the arranged rendezvous point for our trip to the hot springs. We're hanging around for quite some time and no one arrives. We're just about to forget the idea and clear off to the tapas bars when a dodgy, weathered looking, skinny Spanish peasant appears and directs us toward two battered white vans (which of course we enter without question). Once the driver and his 'accomplice' have us crammed into their vans they set off and ask whether we have brought beer, we didn't realise a trip to the hot springs required alcohol and admit that we don't have any. He promptly pulls over to a garage and orders us out for beer – we reluctantly carry out his orders. The drive continues for quite some time until we're well away from civilization, they turn onto a dirt track and through a field and it's at this point I can see the 'backpackers missing' headline forming and I begin to plan my dramatic, courageous escape. Just as I'm running through the finer points of my plan the vans pull up alongside some cars parked in the darkness and the headlights shine over a pool – we've apparently arrived at the hot spring rather than certain death and I'm more than happy with this.

Surprisingly, a pitch-black pool of water in the middle of nowhere doesn't have any changing facilities so we change out in the open and lock our belongings in the van. It takes a little nerve to step into a dark pool in the middle of the night, but once everyone plucks up the courage it's pleasantly warm and with a clear view of the night sky. We get started on the beer and relax under the stars.

Suddenly a deep male voice out of the darkness proclaims "there are more pools over there", and we all look at each other wondering where this voice is emanating from. (It turns out that it's just a strange man hiding behind a small waterfall who's been silently staring at us for the last half an hour so that's just fine). The next pool down is a little swampier and difficult to negotiate although there are several trees where you can hang your bag of beers – a definite selling point. One of the girls in the group is keen to investigate the last pool and moves further downwards only to return with a shocked expression and the feedback that "There's a big scary group of hairy men down there, naked, or in Speedos, waiting for girls to sacrifice". This prompts all the lads down to take a look, I've already seen enough naked men on this trip to last me several lifetimes so head back up to the first pool which is now deserted (I check behind the waterfall to make sure). I float on my back and stare up at the star filled sky, thoroughly relaxed and enjoying the moment. That is until a fat naked man wades past me and shatters my oasis.

The man in the van flashes his headlights: its 1am and time to return to Granada (from wherever we are). On returning to the hostel and light, we discover that we are all (and subsequently our clothes) covered in red clay and smell really quite badly. I contemplate having a shower but the fear of kidnap, relaxation and beer has made me quite tired and I retire to my bunk. I'm abruptly awoken at six in the morning by the loudest snoring I've ever heard in my life: the chap in the bunk next to mine is laying flat on his back with his head tilted backward – the premier snoring position. I poke him with my finger but this has absolutely no effect, and so try shaking him by the arm - nothing again. I prod the walrus with my water bottle before whacking him on the chest with it. None of this stirs him at all so I wrap a pillow to my head – It fails to soften the din so I give up and arise to go and queue up to buy tickets for the popular Alhambra, still half asleep and forgetting that 1) I'm covered in clay and 2) I smell terrible.

Tapas

After a lovely day at the Alhambra, the evening's activity is something else that I've heard much about and not yet sampled – the famous Granada 'free tapas'. There are plenty of establishments offering this throughout the town, most notably on two streets - Calle Navas & Calle Elviria. It really is the most fantastic concept - forget all about dinner arrangement, find a bar and order a beer. You will then be presented with a small tapas dish. If you stay in the same bar then the next drink you order will come with a different dish, you work your way through lots of busy bars, meet plenty of people and sample a plethora of different dishes – all in the price of a drink – it's like a pub crawl with free snacks all night, absolute backpacker heaven! I sampled a mini hamburger, bacon sandwich, bagels, fries, garlic mushrooms, brochette, salad, meatballs, cheese, ham and shrimps – you end up having had a damn good feed and a little on the wrong side of drunk. What a town!

13 – Portugal

I'm caught in something of a 'Brit package holiday' trap in Portugal, as my trip to Lisbon falls through, and I find myself down on the Algarve. I book into a friendly backpackers in Lagos and fall in with a fun-loving crowd of Australians and Canadians at my hostel and (reluctantly of course) join in with lazy days on the beach and nights of drunken debauchery amongst the plethora of bars that populate Lagos' streets. British named pubs like 'Fools & Horses', 'Thirsty Turtle' and 'Pigs Head' are fronted by cheeky, chirpy Essex lads handing out flyers for 2-4-1 drinks offers whilst behind them music from the latest 'Now that's what I call utter shit' compilation CD bangs out. It's entertaining fare for a few days but there are only so many days of vodka and red bull/R&B music one person can take before it all becomes a little repetitive and dull.

One morning I'm relaxing at a café, nursing a hangover and about to attack an English breakfast. It dawns on me that I'm sitting nicely back in my comfort zone before even getting half way through the journey – I need to get myself back on track. I pledge that this will be the one and only English breakfast of the trip, and quickly polish it off by mopping the left over baked bean sauce with my toast. I marvel at an entertaining busker energetically singing a fine rendition of his own song (joining in with the fifth chorus) and chuckle at the clearly disgruntled waiter whose technique for clearing tables is placing a plastic washing up bowl on the end of the table, scooping the entire contents off with his arm and sending them crashing loudly into the bowl. I head off to find something to do that doesn't involve drinking cheap spirits, having to listen to the latest track from 'Acorn' or sitting on a beach.

Faro

It's an overcast, grey and uninspiring afternoon when I make it into Faro (the Algarve's capital) the day before my flight back to the UK. I'm not in the best of moods after being stuck behind a couple of American cheerleader girlies on the bus, talking about how 'Corey is like soo hot' and 'like, my dad is totally paying for everything so whatever!' for the entire journey. I've got no accommodation booked so make this the first priority. I'm not enamoured with the idea of traipsing around the place with Clive so leave him in the clutches of an extremely unreliable looking man running the grubby left luggage office at the bus station.

I locate the tourist information centre and am given a map as well as some addresses of nearby guesthouses, there doesn't seem to be a backpacker hostel in town so I enquire as to which guesthouses are the cheapest and set about finding a room for the night. After an hours walking and three *pousadas* (guesthouses) later I've had no luck and am beginning to panic a little. I consider finding the town's nunnery but have a couple of numbers to ring before I fall back on the sisters. The first one is unsuccessful but with the second I conduct a baffling sixty second conversation in broken English with a lady who gives me the impression that she might have a room just before my credit runs out – the address is a fifteen-minute run away and, on arrival, the place looks like it's shut down. After some serious door banging I'm met by the most miserable, tired-looking human being I've ever encountered. He launches a verbal attack on people who don't book ahead during these busy months (he means me) and tells me that he only has three rooms left (can't be that busy then can it pal?). I explain that I require only one room and that now, since he has filled me with sunshine, I'll gladly stay at his welcoming guesthouse, informing him that I'm just going to collect Clive from the clutches of the unreliable luggage guy. My enthusiasm has put him on the back foot and he looks confused, so I make sure to clarify that I have actually got a room – he flashes me a look of disdain and nods – what a lovely man.

On my return to the bus station I arrive at the luggage storage to find the attendant is nowhere to be seen and the door is unlocked. I stroll in, pick Clive up and wonder how many people may have wandered in and helped themselves to other people's bags. I return to the guesthouse and my chum behind the desk wants to know where my friend is: I introduce him to Clive and he's not impressed at all. He reluctantly shows me up to my room, which turns out to be a cupboard with a bed and provides me with a handful of candles, as there's no electricity (possibly). I want to spend as little time in this miserable place as I can so head straight out for a look around the town. There's a lovely little book festival in the square and I laugh to myself – this place is as far removed from Lagos as you can get. There are no kitchen facilities in the 'guesthouse of sadness' so I hunt out some ultra-cheap food – eventually settling on a crepe - more because the place seemed happy and lively than the fact that I fancied a crepe. I eat slowly and stay as long as humanly possible, basking in some much needed happiness, before creeping in the front door of the hotel and sneaking back to my room to avoid the owner's wrath.

14 – Ireland

I travel to Ireland via London and, by the time I've landed at Cork airport and taken a bus into the city, it's getting dark. To make a pleasant change I've planned my accommodation well here and the hostel is only a couple of minutes walk from the bus station. I step into the hostel reception area but there's no one to be seen. There's a bar next door so I wander in there and find the receptionist propping up the bar – welcome to Ireland! I climb the stairs to my room and find a dead/heavily sleeping man in my allotted bunk, I leave Clive propped up against the bed and figure I'll sort it out later. I return to the bar, order a pint of Guinness and chat to a couple of welders working in the town about Irish football and listen to their outspoken opinions on the pros and cons of the local strip clubs – I have to concentrate extremely hard to begin with, as I can't understand a single word they're saying, but after a few more pints I can hear them perfectly. After quite some time (and a fair few pints of the black stuff) I return to the rather cramped dorm room - which is very smelly indeed. I wonder if the dead man who was on my bed (and is no longer there) has been hidden somewhere in the room and is now decomposing. I detach my sense of smell, decide to sleep fully clothed, as I'm fairly sure the sheets haven't been changed, open the window and try to get some sleep despite the sound of a nuclear generator whirring in the background.

Blarney

I'm awoken early the following morning by the sound of cars splashing through Cork's rain soaked streets and rise to grab the complimentary hostel breakfast of cereal and toast. Whilst I'm enjoying a nice cup of tea I overhear a chap on Irish Breakfast TV stating 'There are two lovely pups' and on venturing toward the bus station glimpse a bus headed for what looked to be 'Knockerama' (may have been Knockraha) – I wonder if I'm about to have a day based around comedy names for breasts – I certainly hope so. I'm headed to Blarney today but have missed my bus (due to not being able to locate the bus stop), so I have to settle for an open-top bus tour around Cork and onto Blarney instead. I really don't like the shackles of organised tours but sometimes there's just no other option. We roll through Cork city with our driver 'John' who sounds distinctly like a Londoner to me. I sit up top but it looks like it may rain, and so perch near the steps downward in case I need to make a dash for a seat under cover. I learn that the redevelopment of the bus station cost six million Euros and that a chap named Father Matthew conducted a nation-wide campaign against alcohol and had a statue erected in his honour. We roll past the English markets, the River Lee (and the Shopping trolleys within it) and lastly, St Anne's church, which is topped by a twelve-foot golden fish and has a four-faced 'liar' clock (all of the times are wrong for some reason – not very useful).

We set out on the open road and make our way to Blarney and its famous castle. After paying my entrance fee I stroll along the paths leading to the castle, surrounded by lush green lawns and trees. On reaching the base of the tower I notice what may or may not be the dungeons. Kids are disappearing inside (which is slightly worrying) and there are some other dark passageways underneath so I go and investigate, finding little more than litter (and an old man who said he'd been lost in the castle's bowels for eighty years – I left him to it). As I wait in line with fellow tourists for my opportunity to 'kiss the Blarney stone' I wonder if the rumour that drunken locals sneak into the castle grounds at night and take part in the historic tradition of 'pissing the Blarney Stone' is true (if they're not sneaking in then they're paying the admission fee which is certainly an expensive practical joke). I figure that Guinness has plenty of nutrients in it anyway, so I am more than happy to get stuck in.

Legend has it that if you kiss the Blarney stone, you will receive the 'gift of the gab' in return (I clearly already possess this so it was a bit of a wasted trip). On approaching the 'kissing area' I ask the chap in front of me if he'd mind awfully taking a photo of me, and he angrily refuses before walking off and not kissing the stone – he can only have queued up especially to have a disagreement with a stranger at the top. I'm lowered over the edge of the tower by a cheerful chap in a fetching, woollen sweater, managing to tie a reef knot in my spinal column during the un-natural act of being bent over backwards and kissing a slab of stone (which may or may not have been pissed on) which is an added bonus.

I have a walk around the nearby gardens and find several interesting ancient rocks; I didn't have a guidebook so am unable to tell you the legend behind the 'Witches Kitchen' or the 'Wishing Steps' (although I did perform an Irish jig down the latter whilst wishing for good health for the remainder of my trip – with the way things turned out this was obviously not the way to do it). The dull, overcast weather turns into warm sunshine and I shed my warm clothing, buy a pint of Guinness and find a nice spot on the lawns to eat my packed lunch. The journey back on the open-topped bus is a pleasant affair with John helpfully pointing out a Chelsea pub on the way back into Cork city centre – useful local history.

I have a little time left in the day and, glad to be left to my own devices again, I go for an amble around Cork. I walk up to St Anne's Church to study these 'liar clocks' and the bloody great golden fish at closer quarters and a bell-ringing practice is in session. 'Abide with me' is resounding around the vicinity but if I'm honest it needs a little more work (by 'a little' I mean 'a lot'). I stroll downhill through narrow alleyways, crunching broken glass underfoot and discovering that 'Whitney luvs Dean' – good to know. I end up walking away from the main streets and unearth some colourful little stores and have cheerful exchanges with a couple of locals. I just have time to dive into the English Markets with my new found love of a good market, purchasing an apple from a giant of a man with the biggest hands in the world - like dinner plates they were.

Killarney and The Ring of Kerry

My bus to Killarney tears through country lanes, steaming past the greenest fields I've ever seen (perhaps it's a distinctive Irish shade?). As soon as I touch down in Killarney I know I'm going to like the place. It's a bustling town with scores of colourful shop signs that just make you want to venture inside and buy whatever it is they're offering (two for one colonics, beheadings) and the pubs! There are millions of them (well, lots). I'm hungry so I fix myself another unspectacular meal for one at the hostel (something hideous on toast) and go for a wander. I'm sucked (through no will of my own) into 'Courtney's' pub for a pint of Murphy's and, as I continue my evening walk, the draw of upbeat

Irish music pulls me into 'McSorley's', where three skinhead lads (1 x guitar, 1 x accordion and 1 x spoons) are playing at a frenzied pace. There's a big group in from 'Paddy Wagon' (an organised backpacker bus tour around Ireland), they've drunk every novelty cocktail and shot on the menu and are beginning to get a little over-boisterous, attracting a few concerned looks from some of the local lads. I've had a few pints myself and I figure it's as good a time as any to leave. Some chap is loudly 'pleasuring himself' in the toilet cubicle at the hostel when I return which is a pleasant way to end the evening.

I find the following morning that too much stout when you're not used to it wreaks havoc with your stomach. Maybe it does the same when you are used to it – I'll need to research this.

It's a Friday morning, another overcast day and I'm off on a 'Ring of Kerry' trip. I couldn't find any way of doing the day independently on such short notice so have had to reluctantly book on another bus tour (this one hasn't even got an open top). A chirpy (is there another type?) Irish fellow shows up in a minibus, which isn't spacious enough to seat the people waiting, and cheekily suggests that the females sit on the laps of the males – with a muted reception. The minibus drops us off to rendezvous with a coach and it's with suspicious luck that I find the only seat on the coach with a free seat next to it – something's awry here. We pull away and the driver cheerily introduces himself and loosens up the yet-to-awaken tourists with a couple of gags. 'We're just picking one more up' he announces – cue the appearance of an enormous, rotund Canadian chap in an ill-fitting pair of tight, white shorts (as pointed out by the driver on his microphone whilst he walked towards the coach). He bounces down the aisle toward me and is having trouble squeezing into the remaining seat: "What is up with these seats?" he cries, looking at me for an explanation

'They're not designed for fat wankers,' I want to say but manage to stop myself just in time.

The Ring of Kerry is a scenic peninsula route, west of Killarney. It's filled with greenery, hills, winding roads, spectacular lake and sea views and tourists (I realise I'm part of the problem on this one but I really meant to sort out a bike - honest!). Our comedy driver/guide announces that he had 8 pints of Guinness for breakfast and cracks a few more gags using colourful language that visibly shocks some of the tourists – I think he's absolutely hilarious. He talks of the woman who gave all her land away in Killarney national park to become a nun and admits he wishes he'd married her instead of his current wife. We drive through the town of Killorglin, home of the 'Puck Fair' (where they crown a goat as their king every year – if I understood what the driver was saying correctly) and pause at a Bog Village for one of those annoying sponsored stops that you get on coach tours – I've already spent a day in an Estonian bog and have no desire to see another one, and so settle for an Irish Coffee until I see the prices and stick to my bottle of water instead. In just half an hour, a middle aged American lady manages to get completely leathered on the Irish coffees and staggers out of the shop shouting randomly about how she knows the 'secret recipe'.

We pass Glenbeigh and Dingle Bay and settle for lunch in Cahirciveen. The tour party is herded into a restaurant to buy lunch from a set tourist menu but I'm getting fed up of being herded (I know – I chose to go on this) so I pick through the queue of traffic pouring into the town and head off in search of somewhere with a peaceful view to eat my packed lunch (I'd bought a loaf of bread and some ham and pickle which is something of a treat). I return to the bus and we chug up a mountain, thankfully getting out for some fresh air and a break from the overly chatty fat Canadian, to take in a statue of the Virgin Mary and a viscous wind.

The last stop of the day is in the lovely village of Sneem. They've gone a bit berserk with the coloured paint here and the bright yellow and pink houses are visible from some way away. It's a 'Fairy town,' is Sneem, and at the back of a church sit some small model pyramids which apparently is 'the way the fairies went'. All this confusing fairy talk is making me very thirsty so I head to the luminous pink building that is Dan Murphy's bar and enjoy a pint of Guinness. As our journey nears an end, the bus lurches to a stop in 'the kissing tunnel' and the driver shouts, "kiss the person next to you" – the fat Canadian has just swallowed a banana whole without chewing. 'No' is my unequivocal answer. I'm relieved to get off at Killarney and give my ribs a break from being crushed by the mammoth next to me.

"Good to meet you," said the rotund Canadian.

"Yep, it's been something," said I.

15 – India

Delhi – The Big Con

I arrive at Heathrow airport for my flight to India a yawning mess. I'm selected for a new style 'random body scan' which I'm both excited and flattered about, it involves me making various poses (and slightly overdoing it) whilst the security guy takes pictures in a private booth. Not sure if I prefer it to the build-up and exhilaration of the metal detector but it's a pleasant change.

There are times when I quite enjoy long flights, the extensive movie choice, 'free' meals and the chance to nap at will. That is of course, if you don't have the misfortune of having a screaming child sitting directly behind you - eight hours is a lot of crying. Don't get me wrong, I appreciate that families need to travel and it's a major test for a parent to keep their unhappy child under control but appreciating it isn't going to cure my splitting headache.

It's eleven at night when I touch down in Delhi and passport control is an absolute scrum – a tediously slow moving scrum. At least I'd had the experience of my shambolic visa application at the Indian Embassy in London as preparation for 'super bureaucracy'. I've arranged to be met at the airport by a driver from my chosen hotel, as I don't fancy my first quest in India being tackling public transport across Delhi – especially at this time of night. After locating a man amongst the crowd at the 'arrivals' exit holding a plaque with my name on (the first time I have ever experienced this, I'm slightly disappointed I didn't opt for a comedy name – "Miss. D. Bus" for example). I'm directed to a pillar, where I wait as he scours the airport seeing if he can find a few more people to squeeze in and make some easy money. He fails, and we head off.

We tear recklessly through Delhi's streets. It's warm and I wind a window down only to put it back up when I realise I'm going to need any form of protection I can get. A lorry nearly smashes into the side of us, we hurtle past innumerable *rickshaws* (a little motorised, three-wheeled, private hire vehicle which is a cross between a golf cart and a lawnmower), and horns are blaring constantly. My driver turns and explains, (whilst taking his eyes off the road for a worryingly long while) "there are three laws of the road in India – brake, beep and then look"

"Comforting," I reply, and assume the brace position.

The car slows down; I open my eyes, remove my heart from my mouth and replace it in its correct location. We've arrived in Paharganj and the streets are bustling with people, in short it's chaos, I'm really not ready to face all this and duck straight into the hotel.

I sign the hotel register as requested; a smiling porter picks up Clive (he winces in pain at the weight) and shows me to my room. I'm surprised to be confronted with quite an agreeable room (I'd booked something extremely basic), a king-size bed, satellite TV, a sofa with coffee table and an en-suite bathroom (albeit with a strange colony of tiny insects living in the bath). By now it's two in the morning and all I want to do is go to bed. So that's exactly what I do.

I fail in my attempt to get some sleep and enter the hotel restaurant the following morning a fatigued wreck. Someone enters through the front door and briefly reveals the street outside; it's hot, dusty and absolute bedlam. I order some eggs and am approached by a friendly, old Indian lady who explains she would love to help me plan my itinerary. I thank her for her kind offer and arrange to speak with her after breakfast (although I really just want to go back to bed). During the course of my eating she sends over selected individuals to tell me what a lovely lady she is and how helpful she can be. At this stage, I don't smell a rat, although I wish I had.

What transpired from this point is that I sat with the aforementioned friendly old Indian lady (who was now beaming) in the hotels 'travel agency' (I now recall a worrying lack of official qualifications) and after plying me with hot, sweet Indian 'chai' and waxing lyrical about all India had to offer, I voluntarily parted with (by backpacking India standards) a ridiculous amount of money for what was to turn out to be not a very good guided tour of Rajasthan just so I could go and get some sleep. In summary, it consisted of me being transported in a stifling hot (no air-conditioning), clapped out motor, with a miserable driver (prone to spitting and falling asleep at the wheel) for hour after sweaty, uncomfortable hour. From Delhi, down to Agra to see the Taj Mahal and west onto Jaipur where, after having spent days being herded from one handicraft shop to the next for some hard sell (I do not need a traditional Indian dress shirt or a wooden elephant), I finally decided enough was enough, paid the driver a rather ugly tip and set out to discover the country unaided.

Jaisalmer

I'm not sure why I bothered taking a shower before my night train from Jaipur out west to Jaisalmer. By the time I'd hauled Clive the fifty metres to my taxi I was dripping with sweat again. I arrive at the station entrance and there are people sleeping all over the place (and that's just out in the front of the station). My ticket permits me to use an 'upper class' waiting room (get me!), I have to sign a register and come upon a room with fans and a bathroom area. The floor is filled with Indian families asleep under the fans and I take a seat as close as I can possibly get to the welcome breeze. A teenager sitting a few chairs away stares at me unashamedly for my entire stay in the room; he doesn't take his eyes off me once.

Shortly before my train is due I join the crowd on the platform; everyone is seated on the floor in groups so I plonk myself down on Clive and join them. The train arrives fifteen minutes late, which is not bad at all. I was told to look for a 'reservation sheet' - a sheet of paper with the names of all the passengers located by the doors on each carriage. There are none, so I rely on asking my fellow passengers where my carriage is. I'm pleased to find that the carriage is a nice, cool temperature and nervously set about finding my bunk. Each carriage is divided into blocks, with two stacks of three drop-down bunks on each side of the block whilst another row of bunks two-high runs along the opposite side of the carriage. I locate my numbered bunk, which is at the bottom of a three, and there's some chap sleeping in it. He explains that he didn't really want to sleep in the middle and could we possibly switch bunks? I'm really not that fussed so make my 'bed' as comfortable as possible using the sheet and blanket provided and bed down for the night. Sleeping was difficult due to an impressive display of snoring by the fellow across the aisle - constant, quick-paced and a decent volume. Comfort wise, it wasn't bad at all (despite having to share my bedroom with fifty other people) and once the air conditioning kicked in full blast I even needed my blanket. I'm awoken in the morning by other activity in my 'area'. The bunks are going up and people are taking seats on the bottom beds. I decide to visit the toilet but it's one of those squatting numbers (you place your feet either side of a steel tray and, erm, squat) and I'm not ready to use one of these babies for the first time on a hurtling train. Fortunately I find a 'western style' toilet at the other end of the carriage; I resolve to get some practice on the squat toilets before my next train journey. I return to my seat where I spend the last three hours of the journey being stared at by my five co-passengers, I return a smile. I'm beginning to get used to it now.

Now, I'd read in some travel book or other that arriving at Jaisalmer train station is one hell of an experience. The guesthouse scene there is so cutthroat that hoards of guesthouse owners and touts gather outside the station to try and get business as the trains arrive. I was expecting a bit of a scene as I made my way out and I wasn't disappointed. As you emerge into the open there is a 'safe zone' of around fifty metres at which point several police offers are using sticks to keep back crowds of men holding signs for various establishments and shouting at the new arrivals (at first I thought it was abuse but it turned out to be hotel names). I attempt to make out the name of the hotel I had booked by telephone a couple of days beforehand, but as I edge nearer to the melee, realise that I couldn't see anything. As I reach the crowd's edge, a burly, moustached man without a sign asks me the name of my hotel. I tell him and he replies, "yep, that's me. That's my hotel," grabbing me and guiding me to a jeep where after we've pulled off he admits that he's absolutely nothing to do with my hotel and spends the ten minute journey into town telling me all about his hotel, what a great, clean place it is and how wonderful his camel safari's are. He seems (fairly) genuinely friendly so I tell him I'll pop over and have a chat with him later on.

Jaisalmer is a city of golden yellow buildings (that'll be why it's called the golden city) situated in the desert (hence the camel safari's) - it's over near the Pakistani border if you're interested. The friendly liar in the jeep drops me off at my hotel and, after dumping Clive, I excuse myself from a camel safari sales pitch by explaining that I need to change some money before the banks close. I take a walk around the city and, after changing a travellers cheque, am met again by my friend from the train station who's now on a moped (it's possible he's stalking me). He invites me for a cup of chai (I've been here before) and a chat about camel safaris. I tell him I'll come over in a while. As I make my way back a guy steps out of his shop and beckons me over, after I shake my head and decline he delivers one of my favourite lines of my stay in India, "oh come on mate, you haven't even given me a chance to rip you off!". I resolve to visit his store the next day.

I have a cup of chai with my friend at his hotel and after some bartering (he throws in a breakfast & a room for the night) book on a camel safari with him (not actually with him, he strikes me as being a little large for a camel). I then spend the rest of the day hanging around the big yellow Jaisalmer Fort which (although crumbling) is an interesting visit. Part of the city lies within the walls of the fort (it's over 800 years old you know) and there are some great buildings to see. I visit the palace museum which doesn't really do much for me (I've got to be in the right mood for a museum) but it has great views over the fort and city and offered exhibits such as: armory, relics, furniture, erm, stamps, nicely painted rooms and pigeon shit. I'm ushered out by a guard as its closing time and his running commentary on the exhibits we pass as we make our way to the exit is memorable: "man, woman, camel". Enlightening.

It's a hot, humid night in Jaisalmer. The fan in my room is making very little difference, it's about as effective as an asthmatic child who struggles to blow his candles out at his birthday party, strapped to the ceiling of my room, wheezing intermittently. I'm sweating profusely and struggling to sleep. All of a sudden an almighty storm erupts over Jaisalmer, winds blow through the shutters followed by thunder, lightening and heavy rain. I slip and slide out of my room on the rainwater that's flooding in and take a natural shower to cool down but on my return there's a power cut. My fan has cut out and I'm faced with a sweltering remainder of the night. I wake up extremely dehydrated at six in the morning and nearly attack the cleaner for some bottled water when he arrives. A major part of my time in this country seems to be taken up with sweating and drinking water, I'm not sure I'm cut out for this climate.

A Camel Safari

After my complimentary breakfast I'm speedily whisked through Jaisalmer's streets on the back of a moped. My driver informs me that I'm 'good luck' because I've brought the first rain to the city for four years. This seems a little hard to believe, but I explain that I'm 'the rainmaker' and thank him for his kind comments. We weave through the various piles of animal shit in the streets (at a guess: cow, pig & dog) and arrive at the fort where, as I wait for the rest of the group, I strike up a conversation with a pretty Indian girl in traditional dress who's selling jewelry (her daughter is named Nicola, she has over two-hundred pen friends, taking a photo of her is free and she'll sell me six bracelets for 100 rupees). The rest of the group arrives and we take a jeep fifty kilometres out of Jaisalmer to begin our camel safari.

We rendezvous in the middle of the desert with two men who appear out of thin air and look like they know how to survive out in the middle of nowhere, grubby and tough-looking fellows indeed (which is handy). Accompanying them are five camels of assorted size - the men will be our guides and the camels our rides. I'm presented with my camel, which is heavily laden with cooking gear, food and blankets. After climbing on board my allotted beast and attempting to find a comfortable sitting position (not particularly easy) we trot off into the desert, leaving the road behind us. I nickname my camel 'Dynamo' due to his complete lack of speed and tendency to hang at the rear of the group. Conditions are overcast after last night's storm and it's mercifully cool, we reach some sand dunes after a couple of hours trotting and the guides let the camels loose before cooking us a lunch of curried vegetables and *chapattis* (a flat bread). The cloud clears a little and some sunrays poke through and, once the camels are retrieved, we embark on a lengthy afternoon long trek to another, larger group of dunes in the hope of seeing the sunset. After a late scramble (Dynamo was up to a reluctant trot at one point) we arrive with a few moments to spare and witness the sun sinking behind the dunes. As the desert grows dark, the guides build a fire and prepare dinner; the beds are made (some mattresses and blankets placed on the sand) and as a cool wind passes across the dunes we feast on as much *dhal* (a lentil and spice sauce) and chapattis as we can eat. There's not an awful lot to do in the desert in the night so we lie on the beds beside the fire, staring up at the stars that can be seen through the clouds, reflecting on a good day's safari and drifting off to sleep.

Now then, a couple of unexpected events occur during my night out in the desert. Firstly, I, and the rest of the group, are regularly attacked by gangs of marauding dung beetles. You hear the little buggers hovering toward you in the dark and then feel them touchdown and begin crawling on your skin, frantically grabbing them and flinging them off brings temporary relief until the next wave of attack. Secondly, another heavy storm arrives out of the blue and, as there's no shelter, I have to retreat under a sandy tarpaulin at three o'clock in the morning surrounded by soaking wet mattresses that stink of camel, with five other people (one of whom farts profusely). The rain becomes torrential and the smelly, sandy, cramped, temporary shelter (sheet) becomes a sweaty pod devoid of humour. Escape is impossible for five fun-filled hours.

Daylight finally arrives after what seems an age and miserable, aching individuals emerge from under the tarpaulin one by one. It feels good to walk and breathe fresh air and the (now lighter) rain provides a chance to wash off some of the sand that's clinging to our clammy skin. The rain peters out and the guides make breakfast for the dishevelled group. Within the hour we're slapping on sun cream, as the sun has reared it's head, and we're getting absolutely frazzled. The rest of the day is a sun-baked trek (I discover that my anti-malarial tablets don't mix well with the sun and I've turned an attractive shade of red) back towards civilisation, stopping briefly under a tree for some shelter from the sun and lunch (it transpires that the tree houses an ant colony which is a result). The remainder of the journey is made in near silence, as everyone is tired, sunburned, and sweaty and caked in sand. It's a huge relief to see the jeep when we reach the roadside – it's been an experience but bloody tiring, my bones ache, my arse is bruised and I really need some sleep - unfortunately I have a train tonight!

The cold shower I have on returning to the hotel in Jaisalmer will go down as one of the greatest in my life. I put on some clean clothes and feel like a new man, time to move on...

Jodhpur

I'm transported back to the train station in a rickshaw that the owner has decorated like a temple – I compliment the driver on his sterling effort. Six hours later (a short journey by Indian standards), at five in the morning, I'm in Jodhpur – 'the blue city'. After finally strolling into my chosen hostel (a helpful rickshaw driver had taken me to a completely different one of his choosing to try and make some commission and I'd walked off) and waking up the security guard, he shows me to my room and I try and catch a few hours sleep.

On awaking mid-morning I make for the imposing 'Mehrangarh Fort', which towers over the rest of the city. It's immense, and I climb a slope to locate the fort's entrance. On the way upward I find a stairway that leads up to a lookout tower and clamber to the top to be confronted with an amazing view over the city. You don't really notice all the colours when you're down in the labyrinth of the city streets but when you're high above them it's a striking sea of blue-painted buildings. I arrive at what is evidently the back entrance and search out the ticket office where I'm given a pair of headphones and a cassette player for the audio tour. I'm just beginning the tour and fiddling with my headphones when, out of the blue (get it?), an Indian family mobs me. After we get the obligatory 'hellos', 'What is your good name sir' and handshakes out of the way I'm surprised to find that the father wants me to autograph his admission ticket. I'm fairly puzzled but am enjoying the odd situation so go ahead and sign his ticket. I am then requested to sign all of his children's hands and some rupees that the mother was holding before they thank me, happily wish me a good day and go on with their visit. To this day I've not the faintest idea who they thought I was.

The fort (it's never been taken by force you know) is a fascinating place: I hear a tale of a man who was sealed alive in the walls to break a 'scarcity of water curse' (unlucky fellow), there are handprints from the wives of dead Maharaja's, palaces, a coronation chair, lot's of weapons and cannons, intricate paintings depicting demons and gods, and there's even a lounge where you can pause, rest and have a cold drink. Whilst I'm doing just that and taking in more of the great views the doorman pops over to ask me if I need any opium. I let him know that the fanta will suffice for the time being and he returns to his post.

I head to 'Jaswant Thada', which is a memorial to Maharajah Jaswant Singh (1873-1895). It's Jodhpur's very own 'Taj Mahal' (although with a lot less tourists): a large white monument with small gardens sitting by a green lake, offering fine views across to the Mehrangarh. I have a look inside the quiet monument and then chill out on the gardens for a short while. On exiting, I decide to take a drink from the stall at the entrance and come across arguably the strangest man in India:

"Where are you from sir?" he asks.

"England," I reply.

"English men are very handsome."

"Yep," he has a point, we are. Everything seems OK so far.

"English girls are like Indian girls..."

"Really?"

"Are you married?"

"No." – still fairly standard banter.

"Do you have a karma sutra?"

"No, I don't." – getting slightly stranger.

"I really don't like fat women you know? I like them nice and thin. They have lovely small vaginas, the little girls..."

"Oh really?" – Where on earth is this conversation going?

"I compared penis size with an English guy who visited here once you know; we were a very similar size..."

"My God, I really have to go!"

"Do you have any gift you could leave for me? I collect pens, sunglasses and perfume…"

"Erm, no. No I don't, goodbye!"

I walk quickly toward the street (looking over my shoulder to make sure the strange man isn't following me with something dangling out of his trousers) and leap into the first rickshaw that passes. It happens that it's already full with a family of five and I hang out of the door (and on for dear life) as we career down the hillside and back into the city.

The following afternoon (I know, I'm trying to catch up on my sleep) is spent at the city's markets. I want to buy some Indian chai to send home (for it's magical powers of persuasion) and had been recommended an excellent spice shop to visit by my hostel owner (who had also tried to buy my mobile phone). I discover that there are an awful lot of spice shops in the market and they're all similarly named (apparently, when one shop becomes popular with travellers they all copy the name and you're confronted by several identical stalls). It takes me quite some while to find the one I'm searching for, and I locate it just in the nick of time as a storm breaks out over the city. I duck in, introduce myself and shelter inside the shop for over an hour. I'm shown the ins and outs of the spice world by a pretty girl (one of seven sisters) in her late teens. She shows me how to spot the fake saffron that's offered in the markets (it's made of newspaper and chapatti mix apparently), I try various types of tea and chat to the girls about their family business until the rain halts. I leave with some chai, curry spices and a cookbook.

Now, no trip to Jodhpur is complete without a visit to see the fantastic 'Omelette Man'; he's been made famous by a previous recommendation in the Lonely Planet guidebook and is now a cult figure in backpacking circles. I locate his stall on the outskirts of the market, check that he actually is 'the' omelette man (rather than an impostor), introduce myself and order one of his recommended specials. The rain starts up once more and a power cut kicks in. I shelter under a dripping canopy on the step of a nearby shop as the Omelette man is busy at work, he brings over an 'egg masterpiece' complete with hot curry sauce and I hungrily devour it before leaving a favourable comment alongside hundreds of others in his 'omelette guestbook'. I thank the Omelette man for the meal, pose for a photograph and depart - a tasty end to an enjoyable stay in Jodhpur.

Varanasi

The longest train journey of my stay in India, to the holy city of Varanasi, leaves Jodhpur at nine in the morning. I'm sharing my compartment with a fascinating seventy-year-old retired judge travelling to Jaipur. We talk of the differences between the family set up in India and in the UK for quite some time (there are an awful lot of differences to discuss!). I'm later joined by a couple with a crying child who miraculously stops every time he looks at me. The next three hours consists of the child crying and the parents using my novelty value and thrusting him toward me until he stops. I feel thoroughly used. The fun ends when the bunks start to come down at nine in the evening and the busy carriage prepares for the night. Shortly after, my night preparations are complete, my bed is nicely made and I've taken my bunk. A group of four Indian lads in their twenties board the train and explain that they only managed to get three bunks together, and their friend has to sleep in a block all on his own - would it be possible for me to move so that they can all be together? I'm not one to be responsible for male friends sleeping apart so agree to vacate my carefully made bed and move bunks.

My most successful night's sleep on an Indian train passes and, on awakening during mid-morning (everyone else has evidently been awake for quite some while and packed up their bunks), the dry, dusty land has disappeared and been replaced with green fields, trees and rivers. Someone said to me that "India is a country of many countries" and I would certainly agree. It's also absolutely bonkers.

There's a very strange occurrence at the Varanasi train station – an honest rickshaw driver, he directs me to the tourist office (I was expecting to be told it's burnt down or disappeared – normal practice in India) and then slashes his asking price when I explain the woman in the office has informed me what I should be paying for a rickshaw fare. I'm taken to my chosen hotel (rather than his brothers) and welcomed warmly by the proprietors. All this genuine kindness puts me in a trusting mood and as my body has been thoroughly knotted from being seated on trains for much of the last few days I agree to a massage from a strange looking, small, silver haired man.

It all seemed like a good idea half an hour ago. Now that I'm confronted in my room by the aforementioned fellow, who's wearing nothing but a well travelled pair of boxer shorts, it doesn't seem like such a great call. Despite my doubts, I bite the bullet, lay face first on the bed and brace myself. He spends the next forty minutes walking on me. There's some punching, he uses various weapons and oils, a rolling pin? A squash ball? Some kind of wire brush on the soles of my feet, perhaps a hammer? Then all of a sudden he's done and asks if I can write a recommendation for his services on the back of my room door (which confuses me even further). He leaves me standing in my pants looking extremely perplexed (and oily) whilst handing me his business card.

I rent a man and his knackered rickshaw and head for Sarnath (another holy town) which is around ten kilometres away; it takes the best part of forty-five minutes to get there due to my chosen mode of transport and the chaos on the streets in Varanasi. I feel I must quickly touch on Indian roads here, you couldn't make it up: cars, trucks, rickshaws (auto & cycle), motorbikes, mopeds, cycles, cows, dogs, goats, people, elephants (and a fair amount of shit) all share the tiny little dusty roads and there are no rules - absolutely none (oh, apart from beep your horn a lot). It's utter carnage. The thing is, you'd think that this would make for a melting pot of anger and conflict but there's no such thing as road rage here; everyone just gets on with it without batting an eyelid. I thought about starting off a 'domino effect' with a quick hand sign that would sweep good old British road rage through the country and start a civil war but decided better of it. It takes long enough to get anywhere as it is...

I visit a temple (Hindu I think), the local archaeological museum that contains lots of Buddha remnants and then walk to the enormous 'Dhameskh Stupa', which is an immense Buddhist monument (imagine a massive great stone thimble the size of a three storey house). A monk of some type walks alongside me and informs me that these grounds are where Lord Buddha gave his first sermon. I try to thank and escape him but he won't go away, which indicates he probably wants some money. I offer him a tip but he tells me that my payment for guide services I didn't even ask for is not nearly enough and I should pay more. Is a holy man allowed to do that? Is he a holy man? Perhaps he's just a chap dressed in an orange bed sheet trying to make a few quid.

I'm due to take part in a sunset boat ride along the Ganges river (aka the Ganga) and am led down to a nearby *ghat* (groups of steps that line the river) to board my rowing boat. After previously reading how heavily polluted the water in the Ganga is, I'm afraid to get any of it on me. As darkness falls a human corpse is pointed out floating in the water. (I knew people came here to be cremated but didn't realise that bodies were left in the river! Blimey!). At one of the main ghats a ceremony is taking place – 'Ganga Puja'. I'm told this ceremony takes place each evening and involves incense, smoke, fire, clapping and a power cut, which takes all the lights out. I buy a floating candle to place in the river 'for good karma' from one of the kids hopping the boats selling them. It sinks instantly (I wonder what that means?). I'm also shown a 'burning ghat' further downriver where cremation takes place – this is one complex city...

Apparently there's only five hours of electricity a day in Varanasi. As I don't know whether this is a temporary or permanent measure, I question this and am told that it has 'something to do with politics'. I have a lizard in my room; I've adopted him as a pet and named him *'baksheesh'* (meaning gift/tip – something you're asked for an awful lot in India). After a little sleep I'm awoken at five in the morning for the sunrise boat trip. Now you can really see the Ganga in all its mystic glory and, along with the fiery dawn sky, this makes for an awesome sight. The wind is up and the river is awfully choppy, the locals are out at the ghats in force - bathing, washing, doing their laundry, cleaning dishes and some are swimming (you wouldn't catch me doing that). Our boatman washes his mouth out with the murky water and I wince; it's amazing what a bit of belief will do for you; men sporting a dazzling assortment of 'tanga briefs' bathe near the ghats and the 'burning ghat' is busy being stocked with fresh wood. As our boat turns back, three bodies wrapped in material are lowered into the river and immersed before being carried back up the steps. I scour the water for more corpses as we head back but there are none bobbing around on this morning.

I then embark on a sightseeing tour with a twist - on the back of a motorbike driven by my hotel's resident pervert. He races around the streets, stopping occasionally to stare at a woman (looking at me for encouragement) and covering us in dust as we career somewhat dangerously through the windswept city. We visit the Benaras Hindu University (where I make a call at the Vishwanath Temple) and the Bharat Kala Museum (guarded by the most miserable people in the world), which houses historical sculptures and paintings. We must have been running late for a pre-arranged handicraft shop appointment as a couple more temples whiz past and we arrive in the Moslem neighborhood. The bike wobbles through the narrow streets and we arrive at a house where I'm given a tour of a silk weaving establishment and then shown to a room with a cushioned floor and given the full show. I purchase a silk scarf for my mother just to get the hell out: I've run out of believable excuses for escaping handicraft shops by now and buying something cheap saves an awful lot of time and energy.

I'm awoken the next morning by rain and prepare for the yoga lesson I've booked for this morning. The yoga 'guru' shows up and treats a Canadian girl and myself to a decidedly half-arsed lesson in someone's poky bedroom. You couldn't swing a kitten in this room so it certainly wasn't big enough for a yoga class for three. What followed was classic comedy involving standing on the beds (who needs mats?), me smashing various limbs against the wall and then knocking a clock off it. Not particularly relaxing or spiritual – just funny. I did discover that I have absolutely no flexibility whatsoever though.

So, my time in India swiftly comes to an end and I'm thoroughly exhausted. The people here are impossible to fathom, 90% love you and the other 10% hate you. Unfortunately, of the 90%, 40% love you because they want you to buy whatever it is they're selling (saris, rugs, paintings, some old wooden tat, accommodation, guided tours, postcards, trips - you name it, they're trying to flog it). One thing is for certain, no matter where you are, or what time of the day it is - someone is going to want something from you. Peace and quiet is not an easy thing to come by (not in Rajasthan or Uttar Pradesh anyway). You soon get used to the staring (there's a lot of that) and learn that it's out of curiosity rather than rudeness. I seem to have inherited a large amount of family during my time here (at least 25 brothers): It's amazing how just staying at someone's guesthouse or eating a meal at their restaurant (I'm actually sick of Indian food - never thought I'd say that) propels you into their family circle. I even have a marriage arranged in Jodhpur, which I'm going to have to cancel at some point.

No amount of research or preparation can set you up for the battering of the senses that India provides. Manic, confusing, but worth every minute – writing about it doesn't do it justice; you have to experience it to believe it.

16 – Hong Kong

Now, some would argue that Hong Kong isn't technically a country (several people tried during my trip and were struck off my emailing list). It's an SAR (Special Administrative Region) with immigration, passport stamps & customs so it's damn well in as far as I'm concerned – and we'll hear no more of it.

I have to admit I was laughing insanely (in the style of a cartoon villain - Baron Greenback of Dangermouse if you will, or Skeletor for any overseas listeners) when I landed in Hong Kong. It must be the easiest place to navigate in the world. For a place that isn't that large (1 x Peninsula, 1 x Hong Kong island and some other random islands) it has the most incredible transport links - trains, the MTR (mass transit railway – that's tube to you and I), trams and at least one-hundred-thousand buses. Everything is in Chinese & English and there are signs at the end of every street telling you exactly where you are and where you want to go next.

So you can imagine after the unpredictable insanity that was India, it's a pleasant change to be a 'townie' for a few days and feel a little at home (apart from I am living in the enormous shopping centre that is Causeway Bay instead of round the corner from one of the South of England's most notorious council estates). I touch down fairly late in the evening on a flight from Thailand and am whisked from the airport in a futuristic, talking, double-decker bus. I may be imagining things but, as I take in my new surroundings, it seems that the many skyscrapers lining the city are performing some kind of light show. I disembark in Causeway Bay and have great difficulty locating my hostel amongst the immense sprawl of shopping malls and fast food restaurants, combined with the sheer volume of people walking the streets. I am eventually aided by a very friendly policeman who points me in the right direction (the opposite one to the way I was walking).

My accommodation is an apartment block in which the owner seems to own several apartments and rents them out by the bed, so that you find yourself sharing a room/flat with a mixture of backpackers, ex-pats and locals. I quite fancy a cold beer and, on the advice of the hostel owner (Mr. Wang), head to a nearby basement sports bar that is packed with locals excitedly taking in an English Premiership football game on the big screens. I order a pint and am astounded to find that it cost almost as much as I was paying for my night's accommodation (and there was an extra charge for 'table service' when I'd clearly been standing at the bar). After nursing the pint for as long as feasibly possible, I head back to the hostel with the realisation that I won't be out partying much whilst in Hong Kong.

Once you manage to escape from the maze of stores and chain burger restaurants/coffee shops, there's plenty to see in the city. I visit the 'Man Mo' temple (Man, being the God of Literature, and Mo, being the God of Martial Valour). Built in the 1800's, it's a compact place, with scores of massive incense coils hanging from above, creating a mass of fragrant smoke. Walking through the temple you feel like you've travelled back in time, so far removed is it from its surroundings. In fact, when I emerge from the smoke it's 1955 and I save a man who's fallen out of a tree from being hit by a car, which puts me in a real pickle because it turns out that he's my father and my mother was supposed to nurse him back to health, they would attend the 'enchantment under the sea' dance together, kiss, get married and have me; or something along those lines.

I head for the Peak Tram, the easiest way to make your way up to Victoria Peak but on arriving feel a sudden urge to scale the peak by foot rather than join the tourist hordes, so off I set. As I enthusiastically march off I meet a couple who look in a poor state of health. They have just walked to the top and back and warn me that it's an extremely strenuous undertaking. I thank them for their advice (they weren't to know that I'm a champion hill-walker) and begin my ascent. It's a long, steep, humid walk and I soon realise that my hill-walking skills aren't up to this kind of test. After making very slow progress (and stopping a few times – for the views, obviously) I arrive at the peak (which seems to be yet another shopping mall – I should have known) and make for the roof, which gives stunning views of the harbour and the city. Whilst I'm sizing everything up for a nice photo I'm joined by a group of what appears to be forty-year-old German boy scouts. Obviously this grabs my attention and I watch (with some laughing) as they dig into their McDonald's like excited children (one of them spills sauce on his woggle). Unfortunately, during this humorous interlude it starts to rain and everyone retreats inside the mall. I don't fancy walking back down in the rain (actually, I don't fancy walking back down full stop) so take a bus back to Causeway Bay and am swallowed up into the mad crowds once more.

17 – China

A simple bus journey

Walking across the border from Lo Wu, Hong Kong into Shenzhen, China is like passing into another world. All those comforts you have taken for granted in Hong Kong disappear from sight in an instant. At first glance it appears I've arrived in a country where all is written in symbols and there is little or no English spoken. I have a little time to spare before my onward bus from Shenzhen to Yangshuo leaves and am confident that even someone with my limited intellect can locate the bus station with time to spare.

I notice some coaches gathered under a building in the near distance and this seems as good a place to start as any. It's awfully difficult to gauge whether I'm in the correct place however, as I'm confronted with numerous signs in Chinese. A woman reads my puzzled expression and gestures for me to show her my bus ticket. I present it; she laughs and points me back towards the direction I've come from. Her point wasn't particularly specific and no one in the immediate area seems to speak English so I return back inside the border building and find a girl working in a tour office who speaks a little. She explains that the bus station I'm looking for is across town and shows me how to find my way there.

On arrival at the second bus station I realise that the signs aren't likely to assist me and adopt the same quizzical look in the hope that another kind woman might come to my aid. This works like a charm and I soon have a couple of smiling ladies leading me by the arm down the road to a third bus station which I'm confident is the correct one. My 'hold your ticket and make a puzzled face' tactic causes absolute chaos here as people rush to help me, all offering advice in Chinese and still leaving me with no idea where to locate my bus with time quickly running out. One kindly chap explains that the symbols on my ticket are the place names, and I spend the next ten minutes parading up and down the bus depot comparing the symbols on my ticket with those on cards in the front of the bus windows, like some mad game of mah-jongg. This tactic (although much fun) proves unsuccessful and I am soon ushered out of the parking area by an official who, after seeing my ticket/face combo, points me towards the ticket office. They tell me something and point a couple of times over my shoulder. I have absolutely no idea what they're trying to tell me.

As I made my way back to the parking bays I noticed a girl who looks like a backpacker (she's not Chinese, has blonde hair and a backpack). By some incredible twist of luck she's English, working as a tour guide and speaks a little Chinese. It transpires that she's waiting for the same bus as me and explains that she's just discovered that it hasn't shown up and has been delayed by two hours. I am overjoyed to finally discover what on earth is happening and head straight into the bus station restaurant to celebrate. I choose a complicated looking group of symbols off the menu and wait to see what will turn up. It turns out to be some chicken bones and rice. Yummy, appetising.

Courtesy of my 'likeable stupidity' and lack of foreign language skill I have become something of a cult figure within the bus station. When the bus finally rears its head some two and a half hours later this creates great excitement, and there is applause and several handshakes between my fans and I. I step onto the bus, turn to wave farewell to my adoring fans and am told off by the stewardess for not removing my shoes as I enter. Oops.

Now I tell you, this is no ordinary bus. Everyone is allocated a (very small) bunk with a pillow and an extremely comfortable duvet; I'm a little upset that I'm a couple of inches too tall to lie flat until I look across the aisle and see a huge Scandinavian chap trying to work out just how he's going to cram himself into his tiny bunk. It's a fantastic way to travel: you just lie down on your little bed, switch on some calming music to drown out the manic cartoons blaring out on the TV and watch the world whiz by as you speed through the dark of night toward your destination. Although I must say, waking the whole bus up for a toilet break every two hours is a little overkill.

Yangshuo

Yangshuo is an amazing little town, packed in amongst the feet of some of the thousands of huge stone peaks rising from the surrounding rice paddy fields. My first glimpse of the place is unlike anything I've ever seen - it just doesn't look real. I'm booked in at a highly recommended family 'home stay', where you muck in with the running of the house, learning some Chinese language, painting and cookery skills along the way. The family members who own the place are warm and incredibly friendly and I instantly feel content there, especially when I taste the amazing home cooked food that they provide each morning and evening.

The next few days are refreshingly active; I spend memorable days biking, caving, swimming, climbing and walking in the stunning surrounding countryside whilst nights are filled drinking ice cold 'Tsingtao' beer in the town's backpacker-friendly bars and wandering in marvel around the insane night market. It's a wonderfully atmospheric place; the locals set out tables and chairs and try to entice passersby with a selection of live 'foods' that can be cooked before your very eyes. Bloody great fish swimming in plastic washing-up bowls, eels, chickens (and their feet – they certainly weren't live), river shrimp, something that looks like scorpion, even what seems to be a flattened mouse – possibly peeled off the street only moments before.

One evening, just as I'm admiring the still-living spread laid before me, one of the fish tries to make a desperate 'run' for it and springs out of its bowl onto the road. I gasp in amazement and begin to cheer its unlikely sprint for freedom across the dusty concrete before the stall owner puts a stop to the fun, mistakes my enthusiasm for the escape as enthusiasm for dinner and begins to prepare the poor blighter for my delectation. I try and explain but the message is not getting through to the keen chef so I beat a hasty retreat. Walking through the market, feeling the heat of the stoves, smelling the spices (and occasionally getting some in your eye or down your throat) and becoming enveloped in the buzz almost tempts me to try something ridiculous - even though I was absolutely stuffed from another huge meal at the home stay. I take a sudden blast of spice to the eyeball however, and stagger in some pain out of the market area and away from the mayhem.

Laundry – The traditional way

I've got a huge pile of laundry to do (having not been able to afford a service wash in Hong Kong) and have got to the stage where I can't put it off any longer (everything I own stinks and I'm wearing nothing but a pair of socks). Having explained this to the owner of the home stay, I'm directed to a nearby well where I'm welcomed by a group of giggling ladies – I return their giggles with a confident, knowing nod and bring their attention to my bundle of smelly belongings. One of the 'laundry gang' hands me a bar of soap and, after carefully studying the technique involved, I have a bash myself. Unbeknown to me, the entire laundry club have all stopped what they're doing to take in this clown who has gate crashed their evening wash. I don't realise I've become their entertainment until I get a little over vigorous with the soap and elbow the basket full of my clean, hand rinsed laundry, sending it flying into the air and then back into the well to roars of high pitched laughter from the ladies. I fish it all out, start over again and ensure I complete the job with a little more care, earning me a modicum of respect from my peers. It's going to be very difficult to walk away from Yangshou, my surrogate family, the scenery, the wonderful food and my friends in the laundry club.

Spitting

Let's mix things up a little at this juncture and have a short discussion about one of China's finest attributes – the art of spitting (if you're eating you may want to hold fire for a few moments).

Now, I don't know how it's all come about, whether it's some kind of genetic thing, but the Chinese seem to have copious amounts of catarrh. I know they love the old 'death sticks' but even that doesn't explain the amount of gunk that some of these guys hawk up on a daily basis. The thing is, there's no polite suppression of the muck back down to where it sprang from. It's simply snorted (extremely loudly) into one's throat and then projected out onto the pavement/road/person in front.

All this is performed at any given place/time and without any sense of awkwardness/embarrassment (there are actually 'No Spitting' signs in Hong Kong but in China it seems to be fair game). The frightening thing is, even the women get in on the act. I've never seen a woman conjure up some of the beauties I've witnessed in the last couple of weeks; it really is one of the most un-attractive sights imaginable (apart from facial moles sprouting long beards but that's a topic for another time).

Night Train to Beijing

After spending a few days in Xian (predominately to visit the fascinating terracotta warriors), I make for Beijing on an overnight sleeper train. On arrival at Xian train station I notice that every man and his dog is carrying a bowl of instant noodles onboard so, not wanting to look out of place, I get myself down to the shop and purchase a nice, spicy looking affair (the container was red). I board the T232 train to Beijing, locate my compartment and greet (nod and smile) a little Chinese lady who's slurping away with great vigour at something hot. The compartment is an absolute beauty: lace curtains, doilies and a rose in a little vase on the bedside table; even a bloody TV! A young guy comes in and seems delighted to see me; he speaks excellent English and introduces himself as 'Alien' whilst he shakes my hand vigorously. I look at him and wonder if perhaps he's got a little confused but he presents me with his business card and - lo and behold! – Alien it is.

As the train pulls away I start up a conversation with Alien, discussing China in general, what to expect of Beijing and music. We work our way through pretty much a whole bakery's worth of cookies and then I'm excited to find that everyone is getting their instant noodles out and heading down the corridor. I grab mine, rip the top off, exit the compartment and rush to follow the crowd to a huge steel kettle at the end of the carriage. I queue and nervously wait for my turn (whilst adopting a confident manner and exchanging knowing looks with the queue) before misjudging the tap's power and spilling boiling water on my clothes but, fortunately, not on my skin. I'm a little disappointed to have looked the 'noodle novice' in front of my fellow noodle eaters but pledge to improve my tap skills for my next trip.

We arrive into Beijing slightly later than planned the next morning and I make for the taxi rank. The queue is several miles long so I sigh and anticipate a very long wait. Just as I'm trying to work out a devious plan to expedite my way to the taxis, I hear Alien shouting my name. He sprints toward me and explains that his father is meeting him nearby and will take me to another location where it's far easier to pick up a taxi. He also apologises that had he not been running late for work then he would have arranged to take me all the way to my hostel. I tell him that I'm a little disappointed but we'll have to make do. We cross a footbridge and walk a short way before meeting Alien's father.

His dad doesn't speak English but Alien explains that they have formulated a plan to drop him at the subway so that he can get to work and then his dad will take me to the place that is good for getting cabs. I bid Alien a fond farewell as we drop him off and, after driving around for a while, we end up in what looks like a university campus. Dad hollers a cab whilst he's still driving and the two cars pull over by the side of the street. I hand my directions to Dad and he walks over to have a discussion with the cabbie. It dawns on me at this point that the directions I have are written in English, the cabbie shakes his head and drives off, leaving Dad on his own, looking bemused and holding my directions. He refuses to be beaten and steps into the street to hail another cab. An English speaking fellow has noticed the scene and crosses the street to see if he can be of any help; the three of them strike up a conversation, concluding with the helpful English speaking chap sketching a map with a few symbols on it, presenting it to the cabbie and giving me a double thumbs up. I bid an emotional farewell to Dad and 'helpful guy' and am whisked off to find my hostel. And find it I do.

The Great Wall of China

I spend two days exploring the tourist trap of Beijing on a girl's, multi-coloured bike (complete with shopping basket, bell and comedy horn). Camply cycling through the *hutongs* (alleyways between traditional houses), walking Tianenmen Square and visiting the Forbidden City. I even manage to get stuck in the evening rush hour traffic and my first ever bicycle traffic jam. I bustle my way to the front of the group, brace myself and pull off with a whoop and a few sounds of my comedy horn as a few thousand others and I continue our cycle home.

It's an incredibly early start the next morning for my visit to the Great Wall. A three-hour minibus trip awaits and within minutes of the bus pulling away from the hostel everyone in the vehicle is fast asleep again (apart from the driver – thankfully). I awake moments before we pull up beside a small house in the tiny village of Jinshanling. We are met by the owner of said house who is willing to offer us: 1) use of her outside toilet and 2) some extortionately priced instant coffee. She's mystified when the entire group of penny-watching backpackers are not willing to meet her sky-high prices and retreats in a huff. We begin to head through some woodland, walking towards our entrance to the wall, hotly pursued by a gang of old ladies offering t-shirts, postcards and probing questions such as 'where you from' and 'how long you stay in China'. I manage to leave them behind by setting a rip-roaring pace and, after some clambering upward, we arrive at a closed gate at the wall.

Following a brief moment of panic where it looks like we may have come on the wrong day, the gate slowly creaks open and a woman takes our tickets before dodging my over keen attempts to get a photo of myself with 'the gatekeeper'. Although it's a misty morning the views are still breathtaking and the first hour is spent enjoying being able to spend time alone on one of the most amazing man-made structures in the world. It dawns on the group that we've got a pick-up destination some way away to be at in four hours time so we all start making our way along the wall. Some areas have crumbled away and require a steady foot; some light climbing and a little concentration but it's not too taxing. On more than one occasion I stop and marvel at the feeling that I've got the whole wall to myself. There are occasional meetings with old ladies gathered in the towers, selling drinks, postcards and t-shirts but they're not overly pushy. A security guard sprints past and then returns an hour later (that's some job) and an old man (he looks well over a hundred) apparates out of nowhere and sets out an array of soft drinks for sale before lighting up his pipe and falling asleep.

As we near our final destination of Simatai, the number of people on the wall grows and the state of its repair improves, making the walking/climbing of it far less hazardous. It's still not overly busy though and doesn't detract from the enjoyment of the experience. We realise we're nearing the end of our walk with time to spare so take a few moments to sit on the wall, have some lunch and take it all in (as well as finally buying some postcards off a little old lady who would just not take 'no' for an answer). The mist has cleared a little and unveiled some amazing views. We walk the last few metres with a sense of achievement and pay the toll to cross a footbridge. There is the opportunity to carry on upward and onward but four hours of walking when you're an unfit backpacker is more than enough (and I think we'd seen the most isolated part we were going to). I splash out on a zip cord ride down across the river and a short boat trip to our pickup point where we're met for the long journey back to Beijing, knackered, smelly and ready for a nice long snooze. Once we finally make it back to the hostel, I have a beautiful shower and manage to drag myself into a comfortable armchair where I slump and finally have the cold beer I'd been thinking of for many hours.

18 – Singapore

Little India

Singapore, much like Hong Kong, has impressive transport links and I quickly find myself in Little India, a busy little corner of the country/city. I check into a popular, lively hostel with it's own bar, boasting that it vends the cheapest beer in Singapore. I decide this is worth investigating further and, after being allocated my bunk for the night (in a huge dorm, it must house about sixteen people), take a stool outside by the bustling street and have a nice cold Tiger beer - sensational! It's not long before a few others decide to escape the humidity and have a drink and the growing crowd is informed by one of the hostel workers that there's a 'parade of light' on this evening which is supposed to be a good watch. We set off to find said parade and somehow end up in the middle of a completely different ceremony in a Hindu temple. We receive a few quizzical looks from the ceremonies participants and return sheepishly to the hostel for some more beer.

I'm in possession of a stinking cold and a hangover the following morning and receive a couple of dirty looks from my dorm neighbours to suggest there's a good chance I was having a bit of a snore last night. After stocking up on some fresh fruit to try and give my immune system a helping hand (after giving it a good kicking with beer the previous night) I head off to see what Singapore has to offer me.

I'm really impressed with Singapore's MRT (the metro); it's clean, cheap and very easy to use. I start off at Orchard Road, a leafy shopping boulevard with some seriously sizeable malls, I check out all the expensive stuff I can't buy and make use of the free conveniences. I spend some time in Chinatown, visiting the market (a bit too much tat for my liking) and stocking up on some of my old favourite sweet delicacies before making my way to the Sri Mariamman temple - Singapore's oldest Hindu temple. The tower over the entrance to the temple is adorned with many colourful sculptures of Hindu gods and goddesses and is a spectacular sight. I don't spend too long inside as I'm very wary of getting 'temple burnout' with so much of South-East Asia still to come.

I decide it's high time for some exercise so I jump back on the MRT to 'Harbourfront', I'm not too thrilled at the prospect of visiting Sentosa Island which strikes me as being a bit of a tacky theme park (although not having visited there I can't back this up with any evidence) so plump for a walk up Mount Faber (which is a hill). I start to stride up what seems to be the footpath upward but end up in the front garden of a large, important looking house, following a spot of exploration I happen upon a deserted back road. It looks as if it has recently borne the brunt of a typhoon, nevertheless it's cool and rainforest-esque (if that is a word) and with some further wandering I manage to find an official looking pathway, which leads to 'Marina Point'. This area is also deserted, perhaps because the view of the harbour-front buildings, some ongoing construction work and a small chunk of Sentosa Island isn't particularly inspiring. I walk past an empty restaurant and customer-less gift shop and begin to worry that, whilst I was lost for twenty minutes in the 'jungle', there may have been a '28 Days Later' moment and I am now the only person left in the country. Seconds later I realise that there has been no such occurrence and, as I make for 'Faber Point', there are plenty of people visiting the gardens and milling around. The views of the city from here are slightly more attractive but still a little 'industrial' for my liking. I walk down through the gardens and head back to Little India.

It's high time for a treat and this evening was to provide it, I'd read about a bar on the 71st floor of a hotel that overlooks the city and as luck would have it they have a happy hour on cocktails from 7pm-9pm – perfect for a *'sundowner'* (an alcoholic drink taken as the sun goes down). After putting on some respectable clothing (jeans and a very creased shirt – come on, we're backpacking here) I head down to take a look with one of the lads from the hostel. We find the extremely posh hotel, ride an ear-popping elevator up seventy-one floors and take a seat by one of the windows overlooking the city - amazing views from a ridiculous height. If it wasn't for the 'happy hour' (50% off) there's no way we would be drinking in here, the drink prices are extortionate - fine if you're out on the company credit card but not if you're on a less than generous budget. I order a Tom Collins and watch the sunset from the fantastic vantage point. It's easy to tell when nine o'clock arrives – happy hour ends and all the backpackers finish off the one drink they've been nursing for the last two hours and bugger off, leaving the bar almost empty – quite a comedy moment.

Little India is buzzing when we return, the streets are filled with men (no idea where all the women are) and the stalls are thriving. It still not quite India though and lacks that grit and intensity (it's all a bit clean and organised for my liking) so to make up for it I arrange for a meal at a street restaurant, purchase several cows and place them in the centre of the street, round up a posse of stray dogs and instruct them to shag one another intermittently, spread four sacks of 'Rajasthan Road Dust' around the immediate area and pay a local man to urinate/spit on the pavement in front of me at agreed intervals. All of which combined to make for a much more authentic Indian dining experience.

I spend the next day hanging around by the riverside, visiting the posh bars and restaurants at Clarke Quay (walking past them and looking at the menus) and am upset to find I'm struggling to afford a Tiger at the hostelries in Boat Quay as well. I see the statue of Sir Stamford Raffles (which marks the point where he is said to have landed in 1819 to establish a trading station for the British) and take a stroll around Esplanade Park - home to a theatre complex with a prickly roof nicknamed *'the durians'* (a prickly native fruit) by locals. It is here that I'm unexpectedly accosted by a man wearing a big snake around his neck. He enquires whether I'd like to touch his snake and have my photo taken with it – I explain that it's not really my 'bag' to either touch or have myself photographed with other men's snakes before departing and taking in the various memorials situated in the area, including the Cenotaph which remembers those Singaporeans who died in the two World Wars.

I just have time to make a fleeting visit to one of the huge food halls (where there's a fantastic range of Chinese, Indian and Malayan food) before catching a bus to Singapore train station. For some reason the driver seems to think there are two of me (perhaps I paid for the man standing behind me as well) and charges me accordingly. I'm beginning to wonder if I've missed my stop when the kind man next to me (I had paid for him after all) lets me know that I need to get off. I'm surprised to find an old, gloomy station that reminds me of some of the depots in India - lots of magnolia walls and huge, old-fashioned fans. There's a wait to be allowed onto the platform and, once I've shown my ticket and am allowed to board the train, I find a carriage lined with bunks on either side, two high with a curtain for privacy. I can't find anywhere to leave Clive so just lock him to the foot of the ladder and climb into my bunk. Kuala Lumpur here I come.

19 – Malaysia

To the Islands...

I spend a short time in Kuala Lumpur, seeing what little of interest there is to see and experiencing my first taste of the fantastic (and incredibly cheap) Malayan food from the *hawker* (street vendor) stalls. I then move to the cooler climes and greenery of the Cameron Highlands to be eaten alive by insects, visit enormous tea plantations and see a tribal village, which allows me to achieve a life-long ambition of using a blowpipe. I apologise profusely for injuring the chief's wife and decide it's high time to move on.

It's been a while since I enjoyed my favourite pastime of sitting on a beach and watching the world go by so I'm headed to the Perentian Islands, off the east coast of Malaysia. After being informed by a couple of the tour operators in the Cameron Highlands that they'd stopped running buses out to the islands as monsoon season was about to begin I spoke to a couple who had just returned and reported that the weather there was still fine. A few of us from the hostel organise a private minibus and we have a leisurely eight hour drive in a roomy van, stopping at a restaurant which has no running water (a major factor in my decision not to have anything to eat). There is a mass of minivans parked outside, heading in all different directions. As people wander out of the restaurant trying to find out what's happening there's a rush to get on the minivans. There is a major mess on our route as twenty people have paid to get to the port at Kuala Besut and only two crappy little minivans are here to take them. Arguments break out between a few travelling couples and they throw their bags on board and jump in. The drivers spend the next half hour trying to cram twenty backpacks, a couple of guitars and a didgeridoo into the compact vans and then we're all crammed in like sardines, folded in amongst the baggage.

Our driver is an absolute maniac, a real loose cannon. He embarks on a battle of wits with an equally mentally unbalanced coach driver and between the two of them they display a tremendous ignorance of road etiquette and disregard for their cargo, overtaking two or three cars/lorries at a time (occasionally on blind corners) – and narrowly avoiding several head-on crashes. How we make it to Kuala Besut in one piece I'll never know, but make it there we do. There are two boats that one can catch over to the islands, the slow, cheap one (which we've bought tickets for) and a faster, more expensive one. We're informed after recovering our luggage (and kissing the ground to celebrate the fact we're still alive) that the slow boat is no longer available and we all need to cough up some extra cash for the fast boat. As there's no other option, we all stump up the additional fee to upgrade, board the boat and we're off to paradise! We turn back moments after because the crew has left a group of bemused backpackers waiting on the shore.

Perentian Islands

An hour or so later the boat begins dropping off at the islands (known as 'large' and 'small' to avoid confusion); all the backpacker types are staying on 'Long Beach', which is the cheapest option on the small island. We're met a stone's throw from the beach by a little taxi boat which ferries our group onto the shore. There is a short commotion as a couple of girls don't cope well with carrying their belongings for the short wade through the water to the sand and fumble their backpacks into the sea. We're confronted by a tiny backpacker community sprinkled along a beautiful cove, the tree lined back of the beach inhabited by beach cabins and small shacks selling food and drink – the stuff backpacker dreams are made of. After discovering that the more popular sets of cabins in the central area are full, we find a place further down the beach, still only thirty metres from the seafront and absolutely dirt-cheap. All those that have recently arrived on boats are gleefully running out to the sea for a swim as the sun goes down, the water is warm and it's a fine introduction to life on the island. As we're sitting at one of the bars shortly after, enjoying a beer, a huge explosion of thunder erupts and a heavy storm begins, scattering all those groups gathered on the sand to find shelter. Some are stranded and arrive drenched to the bone. We take refuge in a restaurant until the storm subsides before grabbing a hammock and listening to the sound of the sea and the island's insect life.

I awake early the next morning full of life and decide to have a run on the beach. It's a cloudy morning but already warm and after running the length of the beach and back, have a swim to cool off and then reward myself with a huge breakfast at a wooden shack café. I meet a Canadian girl who has arrived this very morning but doesn't know how to swim and has decided to leave on the next boat (there's not an awful lot you can do on a desert island if you don't like the water). With another one of my breakfast buddies (an American surfer) I decide to go snorkeling, but as I'm paying up, a group of Germans sporting skimpy Speedo's show up and my American friend scarpers. In the end, there are enough people to fill two boats and the scantily clad Germans take one whilst I set off with some friendly Koreans. We speed off for underwater adventure; it's been a long time since I snorkeled and I bowl over the side of the boat (nearly capsizing it, I'd forgotten I'm not quite as 'streamlined' as I once was). Under the water there is some colourful reef and lots of familiar clown and parrotfish. I take a couple of slices of bread under with me and am swamped by hoards of the little buggers. We pause at a fishing village for a spot of lunch; a small hut inhabited by humans and several skinny, stinking sheep is the venue. The horrible little things eat the food scraps as they fall off the tables as well as several discarded napkins.

The highlight of my afternoon comes whilst I'm pottering around underwater looking for some bigger fish to follow around. At first I think my eyes are deceiving me but after a second glance (and filling my pants) I realise that I've spied a decent sized reef shark. I do the logical thing and chase after it but its way too quick for my frenzied splashing about and soon gets away. I spot a couple of turtles and some smaller reef sharks before getting stuck under some reef and giving my legs a good grazing. I realise upon my return that my sun block almost certainly wasn't water resistant as the back of my body is nicely frazzled, particularly the spot behind my knees. I cover myself in aftersun and watch the sun go down with some friends I'd bumped into from Singapore whilst supping a sundowner of warm pineapple juice and cheap Malaysian vodka from a plastic beaker – perfect.

As I'm getting changed to go out for dinner I hear screaming from the toilet block and run out to investigate the commotion. A couple of damsels in distress, standing wrapped in their beach towels explain that there's a 'massive lizard' and a couple of 'horrible frogs' in the outdoor shower cubicle (shed). I'm quite up for being a knight in shining armour and let them know that I'll take care of everything. Armed with a mop I confidently march into the shower block and coax the frogs out of the tray, I'm then confronted by the enormous lizard stretching out for a spot of relaxation beneath the strip light. I lightly prod him a couple of times and he reluctantly scurries under the roof and out into the undergrowth. The girls thank me for my heroic act and I explain that it's my pleasure. I have dinner at a restaurant where the tables sit on the sand, listening to chilled out tunes and digging into some beautiful fresh local fish – this is the life!

It's a joy to wake up on the island each day and I'm always up early, taking a run, having a swim and enjoying a long breakfast just staring out to sea and marvelling at my surroundings. My remaining days are spent snorkeling out in the bay; sunbathing and investigating the other, quieter side of the island (I'm concerned to see signs of development that may mean that the 'hidden backpacker retreat' vibe is shortly to be lost). In the evening we take sundowners on the beach and shelter from the increasing rain intervals, enjoying the magnificent seafood barbeques – wonderful spreads of tuna, marlin, prawns and squid. Crowds of backpackers gather around tables in the sand, rosy red from the sun and swapping tales of the day's sightings underwater (or just comparing sunburn). The cabins are like saunas at night and the fan we have been given just about makes it bearable (until the electricity cuts out).

On my last morning on the island I take one last emotional breakfast at my regular eatery, a pot of coffee, fruit juice, fresh fruit and yoghurt, and scrambled eggs. I bid farewell to the chef at the café (he has no idea who I am or why I'm struggling to hold back the tears), walk the beach one last time, pack Clive with my clothes and a generous amount of sand, take a final lounge in my favourite hammock (which now has my body shape imprinted) and meet the taxi back to the boat.

20 – Thailand

From the Perentian islands I head back across to Eastern Malaysia, pausing briefly in Penang before heading into Thailand and spending some time on the island of Ko Phi Phi (another backpacker Mecca). It is here that I 1) meet an American girl who I team up with to halve accommodation costs and 2) become hopelessly addicted to banana pancakes, fruit shakes and the lethal Chang beer (that which gives its drinker a serious 'Changover' the morning after). After experiencing, eating and drinking all that Ko Phi Phi has to offer, we take the boat back to the port town of Krabi.

Krabi

We dock at Krabi's posh port and are met by a throng of taxis wanting to charge sky-high prices to get to nearby Ao Nang and scoff at their ridiculous pricing, before discovering that there's absolutely no alternative and we have no option but to shell out for an expensive ride. There is a spectacular sunset on the shore; the sky is a colourful mix of red and yellow and looks like it's on fire. Several boat owners offer to carry us across the night water to the popular Ton Sai beach for a small fortune but bankruptcy and hunger influence our decision and we decide to find a place for the night in Ao Nang instead. We're approached by a guest house owner who laughs at the price we're willing to pay for a room and explains that we won't find a place anywhere in town for that price. Twenty strides later we find an ideal room for that exact price with absolutely no haggling at all – I think about going to tell him all about it but think he probably knows already. We soon discover that Ao Nang is full of fat, balding middle-aged western men with young, slim Thai girls. Following this slightly worrying revelation, we grab a curry and a couple of Changs before inexplicably booking a trip to go rock climbing at eight o'clock the next morning.

Early the next morning we're picked up outside our guesthouse and taken to a waterside location to pick up a long boat to Rai Leh beach. On arrival, we stop at a climbing shop and pick up all the bits and pieces necessary for a days climbing, including a bollock-crushing harness and a pair of shoes so small your toes stick out of the end. We walk to a picturesque beachside climbing area and are shown a few tips before scaling the rock face ourselves. After a couple of sweaty, arm-breaking hours we pause for lunch at an expensive looking beachfront restaurant. Half way through lunch, a storm appears out of nowhere and the heavens open and show absolutely no signs of ever closing.

The shocking conditions mean that the rest of the day's climbing is postponed and we have a rainy afternoon to kill. A nice, brisk walk around the island is always a good idea in torrential rain, so three of us depart to Phra Nang beach via a path that cuts through the island, past an exclusive looking, fenced off accommodation complex and souvenir sellers sheltering under a rock face whilst their goods are temporarily covered by plastic sheets. I try and shelter under a tree branch 'umbrella' I've picked up from the floor but unbeknown to me it's populated by an army of red ants who are keenly working their way down my arm and tucking in for lunch. After a look around the now deserted beach and once I've shaken off my new visitors, the only remaining option is to make our way back to the restaurant with a now leaking roof and have a nice pot of tea on this tropical beach (followed by a banana pancake). The light begins to fade and our long boat home finally arrives, it parks a way out from the shore which kindly allows us to wade through the water to it and get even more soaked (if that's possible). The sea is quite angry and we huddle shivering underneath a tarpaulin canopy, which the rain seeps through, dripping on our heads and making for a comfortable and enjoyable journey back to Ao Nang.

Ko Phang Ngang

My American friend and I are up even earlier the next morning for a transfer back to Krabi Town, a *'sawngthaew'* (a pickup truck with a bench either side on the back and a canopy covering) shows up and after we jump on board and set off we stop shortly after to pick up three Norwegian lads who are bidding a fond farewell to their Thai girls from the previous night. The vehicle fills to capacity and speeds to Krabi Town where we are due to meet our onward bus to Surat Thani. The muddy parking area at

Krabi Town is filled with buses, we're led towards an impressive, sparkling bus and just as I get my hopes up we are walked straight past that and into a huge, rickety old Mercedes bus (well, it had a Mercedes badge). This bus fills up with a combination of locals and backpackers and, with a short toilet/cigarette stop, arrives in Surat Thani three hours later. We have to take another bus to the port, then it's all aboard the hulking great ferry for any food you can get your hands on – instant noodles (extra hot), crisps, sugary toast and of course some Chang beer. By the time we arrive at the dock in Ko Phang Ngang it's pouring with rain. A posse of taxi drivers leap on us as we shuffle off the boat bewildered and wet and we're all pretty much herded into taxis to the islands heartbeat - Haad Rin.

The roads are already treacherous but the rain has made them even more so, after a few near accidents we arrive in Haad Rin - the town where no one sleeps, home of Sunrise Beach and the famous 'full moon party' that occurs on it monthly. The island is filling up in anticipation of the next party in a few days time, and accommodation is already proving difficult to find. As the weather is appalling, the multitude of internet cafes and DVD restaurants are packed with backpackers staying in touch with home, catching pirate movies or watching 'The Beach' for the tenth time on their trip. We walk (the wrong way) to the slightly (but not much) quieter spot of Sunset beach, and get even more drenched trekking down the muddy roads to a group of beach huts that will serve as home for the next few days. We're shown to a basic (and a little smelly) wooden cabin that's ten strides from the waterfront; there's a smallish porch with a slightly mouldy hammock, which is a welcome extra. We take a seat in the beach bar, wait for the rain to subside and help ourselves to a Thai curry and a few Changs whilst meeting some of the residents.

Sunrise Beach

You don't really believe what you hear on your travels about Sunrise Beach until you step down there late at night and are confronted by it full on. There are many bars spread all along the back of the beach, each belting out it's own style of music from behemoth sound systems at ear bleeding volume, backpackers sitting calmly on mats outside their chosen venue to begin with, having a drink and watching various fire dancers performing at the sea front. When the booze starts to kick in the mats soon become dance floors (as well as the rest of the beach) and by three in the morning, it's all starting to get a little messy. My American friend gets slightly carried away on her first night, becomes absolutely wasted and takes a naked swim in the sea before strolling into a busy cliff top bar with her breasts out much to the amusement of the bars patrons. We manage to get her to stumble, swim and then crawl her way home – a slightly heavier-than-planned introduction to the island, but it seems there's no alternative but to join in.

Haad Rin the following lunchtime is a surreal place. The bars are now playing calming, mellow tunes, soothing the few ringing ears that have managed to make it out of bed. Everywhere you look people are nursing sore heads and desperately searching for a remedy. Some people have managed to make it back to the beach (or never left) and those with any energy are messing around in the sea with lilos and footballs. The rain returns in the afternoon and I retreat to a restaurant, being waited on by a tripped out hippie who may have been stuck here for quite some time. After watching a stunning sunset from my hammock on Sunset Beach, I try to have a chilled evening (not easy on this island), as it's the Full Moon Party tomorrow. I select my restaurant by the list of films they're showing over the course of the evening rather than the food they sell and spend the evening having a few leisurely Changs, catching some films and watching an Israeli chap scoff the entire menu and sigh with disappointment when he realises there's nothing left to eat. The music at Sunshine Beach kicks off again and it's barely possible to hear the film. When I wake the next morning, it's still pounding away.

The Full Moon Party

I'd spent an easy day in the build up to the full moon party. I'd purchased my boat ticket back to the mainland and a flight to Bangkok and relaxed on the beach before retiring to have a snooze in my increasingly damp hammock when the rain showed up in the afternoon. As darkness falls, I take a walk over to

Sunshine Beach to get a feel for the party preparations. The beach is near empty and the bar workers are laying down mats on the sand. Every shop in the town is setting up tables outside full with small coloured buckets, numerous combinations of vodka/Thai whisky and brain melting energy drinks that I'm not sure are legal. I have a meal in a chilled out restaurant, sat amongst cushions on the floor and consume as much water as I can to prepare my body for tonight's onslaught. Some brave (or stupid) souls have already started drinking at six in the evening, I think they're in for a messy night.

The hours between eight and eleven drag slowly and there is a huge sense of anticipation on the island. The 'warm up' bars begin to fill, showing DVD's of previous parties. The drink begins to flow and the noise level rises, as midnight passes the bars empty out and hundreds of people are flowing through Haad Rin's streets onto the beach, past the shop owners who are trying their best to compete with one another to sell their booze buckets. As the crowds flock onto the beach there are people selling all kinds of tat, floral necklaces, masks, hats and neon paint. Our crowd makes it down the steps onto the beach and it's absolutely packed with bodies; it seems thousands of people are dancing to the banging music in time. Lightning is striking across the sky as it clouds over.

Even at this early hour (by full moon standards) there are casualties (probably the lads from earlier) lying face down in the sand. Men and women are using the sea as one huge urinal; those who are swimming in it at the time don't seem to mind much. There are fire dancers everywhere; many are backpackers who have been practicing for weeks in preparation for this night. A 'hoop of fire' is lit and a queue of keen lads forms to jump through it with varying degrees of success: one chap has had far too much to drink and just collapses onto the ring, rolls about in agony for a few moments and then jumps in to the sea to cool off before grabbing a bucket off his mate and getting stuck in again. I'm constantly offered drugs by Thai men whilst I'm back up on the street buying another bucket of the Thai whisky and dodgy energy drink combination that is giving me limitless energy. I lose my friends and dance from bar to bar, from high tempo techno to reggae, moving up and down the beach, bumping into old friends and familiar faces from Singapore,

Malaysia and Ko Phi Phi. I lose my t-shirt and am painted with neon paint - everything is becoming a blur. The sun rises and the beach resembles a battlefield, official looking locals are checking the beached bodies to make sure they're still breathing, like surveying the wreckage of the Titanic. The sand is littered with bottles, buckets and bodies. I manage to stagger to Sunset Beach but, along with several other individuals, I can only slump onto the sand and pass out. I'm awoken a couple of hours later by the beginning of a huge storm and my left leg being eaten off by a swarm of hungry ants. I'm covered in neon paint and am wearing nothing but a pair of jeans; I crawl back to my beach hut.

The day after

I don't believe I've ever felt this terrible. I wake up on my damp mattress; I've not noticed that the whole hut is damp before. I was supposed to go over to Ko Tao Island today but am deep in the depths of depression. Something I drank last night seems to have unhinged me mentally. I hate this stinking, damp beach hut and need to get out, but I don't know where to go. It's still raining, and I walk through Haad Rin feeling completely paranoid and empty; it looks like I'm not the only one: a girl I've met somewhere before calls over and says hello, but my brain is barely functioning and I whisper a couple of words. She looks at me sorrowfully and smiles – realising that I'm not likely to make very good company. I try and sleep back at the hut but it's impossible, I think I've drunk enough energy drinks to keep me awake for several weeks. I've discovered that there's a mountain of used toilet paper under the hut, which may explain the nasty smell. I can't bear to stay here any longer, so I camp out at one of the DVD restaurants for the rest of the day, nursing some soup and watching film after film after film. The town is quiet, apart from the occasional lunatic still going from the previous night dancing past, and everyone mustering a laugh. I finally manage to feel tired and head back to my cabin (I'm reluctant to call this place home). I must have managed to nod off, as I jump out of my bed when a massive storm erupts and blows the cabin door open, showering the room with rain. The roof starts to leak and the sea seems like it's about to rip through the complex, it's so close. I'm genuinely fearing that I'm about to be caught up in a Tsunami but after twenty minutes or so the storm dies down and I manage to grab a couple of hours sleep as I near my departure from the sandy, damp pit I'm calling a bed.

The Night Boat

I wasn't ready for this. I mean, I didn't really know what to expect from a night boat in Thailand, but hadn't bargained for a floating shed filled with mattresses – that is, however, exactly what I got after walking the plank onboard the 'arc'. Around sixty-five backpackers are crammed into this shed, mostly on the floor but a few in makeshift bunk beds on either side of the aisle that runs down the middle. It's like a slave transport boat from way back when. There are strange looks swapped all round as more people enter the hold, inspect the damp, grimy mattresses and wonder what the night holds in store – now this is what I call travelling in style! Just after ten, the boat lumbers away, the lights are killed and those onboard attempt various ways of killing time on the six-hour trip – reading by torchlight, drinking Chang (that was my one), sleeping (the fellow next to me wanted two spaces worth the greedy bastard), smoking and talking. Shortly after four in the morning, we arrive at Surat Thani; I'm half drunk, knackered and it's still bloody raining.

There are even more shenanigans as the tired and moody cattle are herded off the arc and into an assortment of trucks to be taken to a side street. Here we are met by an old woman selling instant coffee and toast and fronting a shambolic operation to 1) get people to their various destinations, whilst 2) not wasting a single space in any vehicle so she can make as much money as possible. Some walk off in disgust after being messed around for an hour, whilst others go berserk. A couple of girls are close to tears after realising that they've been stalled for so long that they're going to miss their onward journey. One thing everyone had in common was that that no one had the faintest idea how they were going to get to where they wanted to go, and that the coffee was shit. I finally end up in a truck that visited two travel agencies, a bus station and finally the airport where, after an initial period of the staff waking up (it was six in the morning), I manage to get on my flight to Bangkok.

Break in Bangkok

I find a friendly, quiet, family guesthouse in Bangkok where I can recover from the madness of the last couple of weeks, and search for activities that don't involve drinking (well, maybe a little). I spend an afternoon shopping for fake brand clothes (to replace those that have been damaged beyond repair by hostel washing machines) in the ultra cheap warren that is Chatuchak market. I roam the city's sights for the day, visiting various temples, including the 'Temple of Dawn'. It is here that I amazingly meet a Welsh couple named Ian & Anna Jones, to make for a catchy storyline entitled 'Ian & Anna Jones and the Temple of Dawn' (I might have made part of this bit up). I stop for a few Changs in the backpacker village of Kao San Road and have to borrow a comedy pair of XXL clown trousers to wear over my shorts (no shorts allowed) whilst visiting the Grand Palace.

Once I have seen all that there is to see and feel refreshed enough to continue my journey, I make my way up to Northern Thailand.

Chiang Mai

I was told it was going to be nice and cool up north in Chiang Mai but it certainly isn't - it's still baking hot. The first thing I need to do is sort out my visa for Vietnam; my hostel can do this on my behalf, but I require a passport photo. I walk into a nearby photo shop and wake the woman behind the desk who's fast asleep. She doesn't seem to know what she's doing in a photo shop and makes a phone call. Twenty minutes later a chap on a motorbike shows up and he seems to know what's going on, I eventually get what I came for.

I have a walk around the town, which is split by a moat; there are an awful lot of travel agents, all offering treks of one type or another into the surrounding mountains, and Thai cookery courses. I visit a couple of temples on the way round, browse some bookshops and, after asking several people for advice on a decent hill/mountain trek, book on one for the following morning.

Trekking

I'm up early for my trek and take a small bag with a change of clothes, leaving Clive and everything else I own to the hostel. I'm slightly worried about this, but it's normal practice and I'm sure he'll be OK. I have a measly breakfast of shrivelled bacon, warm bread and a thimble of orange juice. A chap arrives in a truck and a small group of us bundle in the back; we're heading to the Doi Chang National Park but stop off at a market along the way where I make the sensible purchase of a torch. The roads become rougher and bumpier before disappearing altogether and soon enough, we're on a dirt track. We arrive at some sort of elephant camp and take lunch before hopping on the big brutes and going for a slow (they keep stopping to rip down plants and trees to eat) ride through a section of the jungle and cross a couple of rivers. It's interesting enough, but I'm not overly comfortable with the idea, and more worried about the elephant's welfare. The elephants are fed and bathed at the end, which makes me feel a little better about things – I'm told they're unfit for work and this is keeping them alive. A chap takes a photo of me and the elephant, and then requests a tip equal to a weeks wages; I give him what I feel is the appropriate rate for pressing a button on my camera.

We drive for a short while longer until we reach a difficult looking hill - this is, of course, where we get out and begin the walking. My borrowed old school army backpack/satchel is both over-packed (from trying to guess the weather and allowing for all occurrences) and exceedingly tight around the shoulders. We walk through the jungle for two hours, removing and replacing shoes to cross rivers at regular intervals (this would later make my shoes smell like a decomposing rat) and nearly toppling over several times, digital camera and all. It's a sweaty, dirty business, and when we walk down to a waterfall's edge, the group is glad to strip off and take a dip in the cool water before it dawns that the smelly, sweaty clothes have to go back on and another hill beckons. A calf-muscle-annihilating, two-hour uphill trek follows with the sound of *'cicados'* (an insect that makes a sound like a car alarm) ringing around us the entire time. Toward the end I'm getting quite vexed, as a mixture of mosquitoes, rain and my soaking clothing bring on some serious fatigue and clumsiness. Just as I'm about to sit down and have a good cry, a hill tribe village comes into view and after a wash from an icy cold barrel of water, a warm Chang and a packet of crumbled biscuits from my bag, life never felt so good.

We have dinner by candlelight on the floor of a communal bamboo hut, sitting cross-legged and balancing a plate on one's lap. We drink some Chang, play some cards and retreat to our hut in the air; it's a cold night and I can't remember the last time I had to wrap up warm to sleep. I load on a few blankets and take my position on the floor, having a good nights sleep following the day's exertions, apart from being rudely awoken by cockerels that seem completely unaware of the time – two in the morning is not dawn as far as I'm aware.

It's a lovely fresh morning as our guide 'Pot' (I suggest that he goes it alone with the misleading moniker of 'Pot Tours') wakes us for a breakfast of scrambled eggs, fruit, local tea and some bananas. I'm informed that it's normal practice for these Thai roosters to set off at one and two in the morning before going berserk between half past four and half past five – that's alright then. My calf muscles are awoken instantly with another steep uphill trek and, within minutes, I'm soaked through with sweat again, reassuringly so is Pot (who is the most fresh faced guide I've ever seen; I like my guides like my boat captains – old, weathered and wise looking). We walk for hours, encountering leeches, spiders, snakes, more of those cicados and comedy plants. We lunch on last night's fried rice and bananas and then lose the track and Pot gets his machete out – I think we might be lost. We brush past plants that sting and cut you, I'm constantly slapping mosquitoes on my neck, past a small marijuana plantation and down an ankle-busting track. We see makeshift blue water pipes, this means plumbing, which in turn means a village. We're told that it's near, very near, near, near, very near. Whilst I'm daydreaming about actually reaching this mystery village that never seems to appear, I nearly fall foul of a landslide and am saved by my trusty bamboo staff.

We finally are no longer near or very near the village but in it and are shown to our 'house' which is nicely away from the rest of the tribe - I sense they're not overly keen at having visitors. It's another dashing bamboo number and, as I open the front door, one of our neighbours is asleep and upon awaking, lights up something (possibly opium), has a good smoke and then wanders off to find somewhere else to hide from the wife and have a snooze/smoke. On removing my shoes, I find that I've been keeping a leech as a pet and my sock is soaked with blood. The evening is made up of another candlelight dinner, some lethal rice wine and entertainment from the kids of the tribe. I hit the floor and wait for the roosters to kick off.

The last (thankfully) walk of the trip is a speedy, five kilometres to a rafting establishment (a collection of huts). There's a spot of fairly tame white-water rafting, followed by a trip down river on a bamboo raft (which I'm nominated to steer after a ten second lesson); I manage to steer into the bank and almost sink the bugger and, after some serious haranguing from my passengers, just about get the raft to our final destination. After sitting and waiting for two hours for a lift home, we are driven back to the hostel in Chiang Mai where I'm re-acquainted with Clive (he's fine), and given a room next to the toilet complex, divided only by a chipboard wall. This allows me to hear all the showering, shitting and vomiting that occurs throughout the night.

Pai

On awaking, I leave my dirty laundry with a woman in a little hut in Chiang Mai and take on a light breakfast (I've been told the ride to the town of Pai is a real rollercoaster). As I've come to expect, it's another jam packed minivan and the rumours of a rough ride are definitely true. The passengers cling to the seats as the compact bus negotiates the hilly roads and exceptionally tight bends. We stop at a pre-organised pause by a roadside cafe and are greeted by a very excitable woman who is desperate to serve us noodle soup and snacks. Four more hours of the rollercoaster are endured before we make it to the lovely town of Pai.

I decide it's high time to confront my demons and hire a moped. I've avoided anything on two wheels since discovering, at the age of fourteen, that on mounting a bike, I turn into a kamikaze maniac and gladly free wheel into the path of moving motor vehicles, resulting in two lengthy stays in hospital. There's no space on the hire form for admission of the complete inability to ride a motorised vehicle so two minutes later I'm in possession of a hulking 125cc beast. I fill her up with gas and we're away! Things are a little shaky at first, but as soon as I get my confidence its plain sailing and I'm tearing through the Thai countryside at an amazing forty miles an hour.

It dawns on me after an hour of being utterly caught up in the moment that I've ridden into the middle of nowhere (not very difficult) so decide to stop at the next village for directions. After quite some while, no village appears, so I turn back instead and see if I've ridden through one without noticing during my hour day-dreaming that I was 'Poncharello' from TV's 'C.H.I.P's'. As it turns out, I had.

I manage to get back on track and wind up at Pai canyon. As usual, I'm wearing completely unsuitable footwear for the task in hand and manage to lose my footing and slide down a cliffside whilst trying to get a good vantage point for the excellent views of the surrounding area. I then ride out to visit a waterfall and almost have an accident as I lose control of the bike whilst scooting over some sand, nearly toppling at high (well, medium) speed. I have to go 'off road' to get to the waterfall and it's a real challenge to stay on the bike. There are some fantastic countryside landscapes along the way and on reaching the waterfall's edge I manage to trip on my flip-flops and fall into the pool below. I decide enough is enough; hop on my bike a sopping wet mess and head back toward Pai. It's starting to rain and I take it easy as I don't want to end up walking the bike back from the middle of nowhere. A huge downpour begins just as I pull into my guesthouse and I take shelter for the umpteenth time – I truly am the rainmaker.

Roosters are my new sworn enemy. Between them and some sort of call to prayer ringing out, I struggle to have a lie-in. I give into their din at eight in the morning and find that several of the buggers are gathered right outside my door - I'm convinced they've ganged up purely to annoy me, I'm sure I heard them sniggering as I walked off. I initially set out to find the Pai Hot Springs and surprisingly succeed. They are indeed hot, and there's a heavily tattooed bald fellow sat in his pants meditating in a hot stream, I start to strip down to join him but he doesn't seem too keen on company so I give it a miss.

Buoyed by my success at actually finding somewhere without getting lost I head for a secluded waterfall I've been told of. After an hours driving, the road disappears and I'm riding along a river bank, muddy from rain the previous night. I manage to get some of the way on the bike before arriving at a rivers edge. I can't ride down a river on a moped (at least I don't think I can) so roll up my shorts and get wading downriver (don't ask me why I'm doing this – I'm caught up in the moment here). After half an hour of wading and walking the dirt paths I get the shock of my life when I make it into a clearing and am confronted by three men with guns.

Now, I've never experienced this type of situation before and therefore am unsure as to how you're supposed to greet a group of men with firearms deep in the middle of a forest. With a quivering arse and a stammer in my voice I smile awkwardly at the three gun-toting chaps and nervously ask 'waterfall?' One of the three points me down a dirt track and I make off at great speed, hoping that they're not a) taking aim or b) following me.

I walk for a few more minutes and come across an untended gun propped up against a tree - I think someone is dodging look-out duty. I've no idea what these people are guarding and in hindsight should probably have turned back but feel I've come this far so may as well carry on. The pattern continues for another hour, crossing the river fourteen more times, moving hopefully upwards before moving downwards again shortly after. Time begins to work against me, I'm supposed to be catching a bus back to Chiang Mai this afternoon (and I foolishly didn't bring any water so am 'slightly parched') and reluctantly I have to give in and turn back.

I never found out if I was actually headed toward the waterfall or toward some sort of plantation or whether I got close to either.

There's some sort of conspiracy trying to prevent me from making it back for my bus: various stray dogs block my path and I nearly hit a woman whose Ganja selling tactic seems to be running into oncoming vehicles, a rooster chances it's luck and I almost come a cropper trying to run him over. I somehow manage to overcome the many obstacles on the road and make it back on time to return the bike unscathed; I then soul destroyingly squeeze myself into the minivan and count the kilometre markers down on the long rollercoaster back to Chiang Mai.

21 – Laos

Those magnificent men in their flying machines

On my return to the washing woman's hut in Chang Mai, she looks guilty as she opens her front door and recognises my face. That's because all my clothes are still wet due to incessant recent rain. I smile, tell her not to worry and that I quite like my clothing a little damp. I squeeze a now impossibly heavy Clive into a tuc-tuc, then onto the airport where the extensive check in for the flight to Laos involves a man opening a door and everyone walking onto the tarmac. I fly into Luang Prabang on a tiny little propeller plane run by a Lao Airline who's safety record is (allegedly) so abysmal that they've had to change their name several times (which seems fairly pointless; as far as I'm aware they're the only Lao airline). The engine was so loud that you couldn't hear the safety drill (I'm not convinced there even was one), and to be fair, it wouldn't have made an awful lot of difference, as the plane was about as robust as those polystyrene toy gliders one used to be able to purchase from newsagents back in the day.

We arrive at Luang Prabang airport and there are some serious shenanigans taking place. The entry visa charge is apparently dependant on the day of the week and, as it's a Sunday, an extra 'overtime fee' is incurred. Several of the backpackers arriving haven't organised their visas before hand (unlike Mr. Organised here) and don't have the required cash (although immigration will seemingly accept any currency - Thai, US dollars or their own Lao Kip – they're not fussy). Some community spirit is required to club together and put up enough cash for these guys to get into the country.

Exploring Luang Prabang

Laos has a French colonial past so they knock up a fine baguette here; unbeknown to me, my chosen breakfast establishment has a talking bird. When said bird begins to make polite conversation with me, this takes me a little by surprise, leading to me spitting my coffee and a fair chunk of my baguette across the table, earning a giggle from the owner who must have seen this happen on many occasions. Luang Prabang is a beautiful town, sitting on the banks of the chocolate brown Mekong River. I feel a temple experience coming on, walking across town with one of the lads from the flight to Wat Xieng Thong, one of Laos' most important temples, sitting in gardens beside the river.

We walk around the temple for a while, admiring the buildings, before taking some steps down at the gardens rear brings us to the riverside. We're met at the foot of the steps by a chap alongside his boat who shows us a hand-made pamphlet which, in a nutshell, says that he'll give us a ride across the river so we can have a wander round, then he'll bring you back over. In an attempt to strike a deal, he informs me that I'm a very handsome man (which I know) and that tonight we should pick up some lovely Laos girls for some 'boom-boom'. This sales patter is the clincher and we come to a monetary agreement. We cross the river and find a couple of ramshackle temples but also some good views back across the river and Luang Prabang. A couple of kids lead us down into a nearby cave, which is sweltering hot, dark and full of damaged Buddhas – they don't speak English so I don't discover why they (the damaged Buddhas, not the kids) are down here.

After recharging the batteries with some lunch, it's an uphill climb on Phu Si hill, a big hill in the old towns centre. It is home to some more temples and unbeatable views over the town/city and the Mekong. After a brief siesta (even brief exercise is now utterly exhausting), the town is in darkness and the main street through town has been shut off to traffic (not that there's much traffic in Luang Prabang anyway) and transformed into a hectic night market. There's a side road especially for food stalls with many weird and wonderful offerings. I opt to play it safe and purchase a baguette filled with some sort of paste (and perhaps ham) and two pieces of 'meat on a stick' – a fine meal by anyone's standards. The main attraction of the market is 'handicrafts' (which is a stroke of luck because anyone who knows me will know that I've had a lifelong obsession with handicrafts - I'm particularly fond of hand-made bedding & slippers which are, fortunately, both in great supply).

Word gets around that there's a Halloween party at a place around the back of the hill in the evening (if you're wondering why on earth there's a Halloween party in Laos it's because said bar is owned by a Canadian family) and a few of us attend to become better acquainted with the phenomenon that is *beerlao* (the national beer – revered by backpackers throughout South-East Asia). On entry we are presented with skeleton masks furnished from paper plates and step into a bar jammed with drunken backpackers. The party continues past one in the morning (which is awfully late for Luang Prabang) when the police arrive to shut down the operation and a throng of inebriated, happy backpackers dressed as skeletons fall out onto the darkened streets and attempt to find their way back home around the hill.

Snoring

I neglected to mention that three of us lads were sharing a room with a German girl to split costs. She had asked during initial negotiations whether anyone of us were 'snorers'. We had all replied that as far as we were aware we weren't and a deal was struck.

However, the morning after the Halloween party she is more than a little angry and, as I prise one of my tired eyes open, she is sitting on the edge of her bed, belongings packed, in wait for me:

"You!" she screams.

"Ah, good morning," groan I.

"You promised!" she screams again.

"Eh?" reply I, extremely confused.

"You promised me!"

(We're getting nowhere here) "What did I promise?"

"You promised you were not a snorer!"

(Ah, now I'm getting it) "I didn't think I was, no one has mentioned it before."

"I haven't slept all night, you come back drunk and snore the whole night."

"I'm really sorry about that love, didn't even know."

"Sorry isn't good enough; I'm getting my own room right now."

"Erm, Fair enough."

Not really what you need when you're sporting a massive hangover.

Route 13

I inexplicably arise at five-thirty on my last morning in the town, as I have been informed that at sunrise, hundreds of orange robed young monks make their way down to the Mekong in some kind of procession. Lo and behold! - That's exactly what they do.

'Route 13' from Luang Prabang to Vang Vieng has become notorious for armed vehicle ambushes by rebels in recent years, causing several deaths. As you can imagine, there is a huge sense of fun and excitement when we board a 'Super VIP', big, pink 'shoot at me' bus, with only a fifteen year old boy clutching a machine gun for protection (although I think I caught sight of a sawn off under the drivers seat and he looked pretty handy). The driver is playing 'I'm never going to dance again' by Wham over the PA system and, if things don't go according to plan, then none of us will be. The legroom on the bus is already minimal (another reason why we may never dance again) but the chap in front of me makes matters a little more uncomfortable by lowering his seat back and crushing both my kneecaps; the 'Big Pink Fun Bus' tears through the Lao countryside, stopping only briefly for some noodle soup. The air-con packs up shortly after our lunch break and we arrive into Vang Vieng on a very hot and smelly bus indeed. The trip has gone off without any bloody battles (I wouldn't have minded a little one, just to get some nice photos as a keepsake) and we're emptied onto a massive, desolate tarmac airstrip. A woman sprints toward us and tells us we must stay at her guesthouse for 2 US dollars a night. It's a little pricey but it sounds like a direct order, so we reluctantly accept.

Vang Vieng

Vang Vieng is a compact gathering of guesthouses, restaurants and bars on a rocky road surrounded by hills. The abandoned airstrip is a remnant of the Vietnam War and was used by the US. The town's income looks to come exclusively from the backpacker element, as there seems to be no other type of traveler to be seen. The reason for this backpacker influx (other than a slightly liberal attitude to soft drugs) is chiefly Vang Vieng's main pastime – 'Tubing' (more about that later).

After dumping our bags, we hire some seriously unroadworthy mountain bikes and set off to investigate the surrounding countryside. A teeth-smashing cycle along bumpy dirt roads and stony lanes follows and, once we pay a toll to cross a bridge, we find ourselves at the ticket office for a cave. We decide to shell out (not a lot) to have a look round said cave and a jolly nice cave it is too. An upward climb reveals a balcony at one of the openings, which gives an impressive panorama over the countryside.

It's back on the bikes for more marvelling at the scenery (whilst trying to prevent our transport from falling to bits and leaving us stranded) until the craving for beerlao becomes too strong. We hole up for the evening at one of the towns numerous bars showing films or American sitcoms (known as 'Friends' bars), have a tasty, traditional Lao dish (*lap* – mixed meat and salad served with sticky rice) and discover that Vang Vieng closes down a fair bit later than Luang Prabang – resulting in some pacing issues and being inebriated far too early in the evening.

Tubing

Most backpackers that happen across Vang Vieng are here for one reason and one reason only – Tubing. Excitable hoardes gather each morning outside a shop that rents big tractor inner tubes (don't worry, all will soon become clear). Each person is branded (well, penned) with a big black number (I'm 31), advised to wear lifejackets (which no-one does for fear of looking silly) and are then driven to the edge of a shallow, lazy river. Here, next to a sign politely asking people 'not to piss here', is where you place your tube on the water, sit inside and begin to slowly drift away on the slight current.

That's not even the beginning of the story though; just aimlessly floating down a river isn't likely to draw crowds of this magnitude. Every few hundred metres, a local entrepreneur will have constructed a makeshift dock on the river bank from wood and bamboo and, whilst waving ice cold bottles of beerlao, will attempt to entice the approaching 'tubers' onto his platform using chanting/singing and the lure of an extremely fragile looking jump/swing/ledge/freefall into the deep/shallow river.

The end result is a hundred or so wasted backpackers taking eight hours for a trip that should last two; suffering various tubing mishaps (flying belly jumps onto protruding metal air valves being a frequent complaint), jumping and drinking related injuries and still drifting down the river when darkness has fallen (with no idea of where to get out). Eventually, the tubers stumble barefoot back into Vang Vieng, their tubes hauled over their shoulders. The town's chill-out cafes ring with the applause and laughter directed at those that are still arriving back into the night like soldiers returning from war. I'm not convinced this enterprise would make it past the health & safety committee in the UK

After a night of story swapping, drinking and much laughter with the tubing gang, I return to my room to find it locked and no sign of my roommate. I'd sent him home earlier in the night because he'd gone a little overboard with the 'happy' products on offer and could no longer stand up. There's no way of getting in (after several attempts at breaking in), so I try a couple of the other rooms and find one unlocked and seemingly unoccupied. I decide to sleep in here, but am rudely awoken at three in the morning by my incoherent roommate banging on all the guesthouse doors. I quiet him down, explain that he has the room key and we manage to grab three hours sleep before our bus to Vientiane.

Vientiane

We arrive in Lao's quiet capital city, Vientiane, and it's baking hot. My hangover has kicked in nicely - I've not got a drop of water in my body. One of the lads and I (the other decided to spend a while longer tubing and getting happy in Vang Vieng) are trawling around trying to find a cheap room. We team up with a Swedish girl who is struggling to afford a room on her own and score a triple room in a fabulous guesthouse for only 1 US dollar each. The walls are covered in damp; the heat is stifling; there are no windows and an overwhelming stink of shit. It's perfect.

After a boozy few days with little sleep, I need to cleanse my body and my soul and end up out of the city, visiting a temple in a calm forest setting. I'm beckoned (by a rather large Lao girl) into a wooden cabin offering herbal saunas and a massage. An exceedingly camp Lao fellow instructs me to remove my clothing, provides me with a pink tablecloth to wrap around myself and directs me to the herbal sauna. I spend half an hour in here sweating out the impurities of the previous few days (and months) before taking a freezing cold shower. Whilst I'm sitting in my pink wrap, waiting for one of the masseurs to finish, I'm served tea, and chat with the large girl and the camp man. A space comes up at one of the beds and, as I stand, the camp chap rushes to relieve his friend of his duties and excitedly calls me across. I'm treated to a 'traditional' (painful) massage and my new friend spends a little longer than was comfortable on my buttocks and inner thighs. He invites me to dinner. I politely refuse.

Exploring Vientiane

Rain has fallen overnight and the city is cloudy and horribly muggy. I notice the city's French colonial architecture a little more this morning with a fresh body and mind. I take breakfast at a French café and walk down to the 'Patuxai', which is Lao's 'Arc de Triomphe' (and a big lump of concrete) before making for the bus station to find a bus out to 'Xieng Khuan' (the 'Buddha park') - a park full of Buddhist and Hindu statues, twenty-five kilometers from the city. I ask a local where I can catch the bus from, and he holds my hand and walks me to the bus stop. My forehead becomes a waterfall as I sit on a tiny old minibus and watch it become more and more overcrowded. Once people are hanging out of the doors and windows, a driver shows up and we're away. I'm sitting next to a slightly mad, old fellow with a major catarrh issue and a red, bobble hat. He's either coughing something up or shouting, and tries to strike up a conversation with me; I just smile and think of my happy place. It takes us over an hour on the bumpy roads to travel the twenty-five kilometers and we're dropped right outside the entrance to the park.

The park is fairly isolated; there's a small shack of a restaurant across the street but not much else. Inside is a collection of statues in a quiet garden setting, including an enormous stone reclining Buddha and a wonderfully madcap 'pumpkin of hell' – complete with a mouth that you can climb through to investigate inside. There are some morbid (some may say disturbing) sculptures and a hole at the very top where you can climb on to the roof and see across the park. Whilst I'm up here snapping off a few aerial photos of the reclining Buddha, a small boy starts a conversation with me from ground level. I meet him back down there and he asks if he can practice his English on me. I say that he's more than welcome to but he only seems to have learnt 'you like Laos?', 'you like Laos food?' and 'you like football?' without understanding any of the answers, so it's a short lived conversation.

No sooner have I exited the park then another (even more battered than the last) bus shows up. This one has a broken windscreen and the floor has fallen away at the back, around the wheel arch. Nevertheless, apart from nearly being hit side-on by a dumper truck we make it back to Vientiane bus station in one piece and I celebrate with a stale baguette filled with pate and what looks like Spam. I drench it in chilli sauce to liven it up a little – a delicious treat costing no more than a few pennies. As the cloud has been burned away (or whatever happens) by the sun, and it's a fine, sunny afternoon, I head down to the riverbank to hang with the flies and savour my last chance of beerlao at one of the many food stalls that line the riverside area. The locals are the opposite of us westerners and, instead of tearing their clothes off at the first ray of sunshine; they try and cover their faces from the sun wherever possible. This makes for some entertaining people watching, as those riding mopeds use hands, bandanas and books to avoid the sunlight but increase the chance of an accident. As I finish my beer and the sun goes down, I walk the shore, which disappointingly turns out to be a real eyesore due to the piles of litter from the food stalls above having been hurled down the banks.

I take a tuc-tuc out to Vientiane airport, passing herds of backpackers who have just arrived in town and are going through the same rigmarole of trying to find a cheap place to stay – I consider recommending the 'Shit-Pit', but we're past them before I get the opportunity for a sales pitch. I'm surprised to find TV showing BBC news at the airport and catch up with the happenings back home for the first time in a while. I watch the clock worryingly as our boarding and departure times both pass with no word until half an hour later when we're told that the flight is delayed because of a 'technical problem'. We eventually leave two-and-a-half hours later (I can recite all the news stories word for word by now), and I take two meals (well, sandwiches) to compensate. I discover how these tropical diseases are spreading the world over – the mosquitoes have become organized and are travelling in planes - this one is full of them. It appears that the technical problem we were told of at Vientiane is that the plane doesn't have any landing gear; we just plain fall out of the sky and plonk onto the runway in Hanoi, North Vietnam.

22 – Vietnam

Farting in dormitories

I'm sure you'll all agree: farting in dormitories is an interesting discussion point. My personal viewpoint is that if you are sharing a dorm room with any more than one stranger then you should stick to the rule that you shouldn't break wind unless you're 1) outside of the communal living area or 2) you're in bed and have something to muffle the sound/smell (in hot countries/dormitories this may not be possible). Therefore, option 2) should only be exercised with extreme caution.

Sticking to this stance makes it extremely difficult to find a 'safe place' when living in a communal area and needing to 'pass wind' – I'm of the opinion that some sort of official backpacker charter needs to be drawn up to firm up some strict guidelines around farting, possibly with an additional review on sex and self-pleasure in dormitories/showers and using alarm clocks considerately.

Anyway, I digress. One of my new roommates in a spotless, roomy and comfortable twelve person dormitory in Hanoi has broken the unwritten rules and is blowing off loudly throughout the night with utter disregard for his neighbours.

Exploring Hanoi

I make a major faux pas during my first morning in the city. It's a Sunday morning; I've no local currency and the banks are closed. I immediately detach my common sense and foolishly utilise one of the over-keen street moneychangers suspiciously loitering outside the bank. Amazingly, the old woman pulls a special trick of the hand whilst counting out my money and relieves me of a few notes without me noticing – well, would you believe it?

There's a special way of crossing the road in madcap Hanoi, the stream of motorbikes, people and cycles through the city's roads is endless so, if you employed the green cross code, you'd be stopping, looking and listening for all eternity. The key is to step off the kerb and into the road (very, very gently) and then slowly walk across in a straight line. The traffic just flows around you – its magic (a bit like the old woman's hand trick).

After mastering crossing a road, I walk past the Hoan Kiem Lake (lake of the restored sword). Legend (again) has it that many moons ago, a Chinese emperor was given a magic sword and used it to win a significant battle. Afterward, when boating on the lake, a giant turtle surfaced, snatched the sword and disappeared into the depths. The moral of the story is not to take swords when boating. I carry onto the Hoa Lo Prison (aka the Hanoi Hilton) where the French kept Vietnamese political prisoners and also a prison for American POW's during the Vietnam conflict. Most of the building has been demolished, but there is a little to see and some exhibits but not much in the way of English explanation so I make up a few stories myself. I decide to put my life on the line once more and hire one of the many madmen offering motorcycle taxis. I strike a deal with one chap on a street corner, jump on the back and he roars straight through a red light and into oncoming traffic – I think you'll agree I've made the right choice. I spend the remainder of the day in the 'Temple of Literature', an 11th century university with classic architecture and quiet gardens, a pleasant (and peaceful) retreat from the howling mad streets of Hanoi.

In the evening, I lead a squadron of backpackers (not sure why they were following me, I had absolutely no idea where I was going) through Hanoi's hectic night streets for some Vietnamese food. I didn't think it would be possible for the city to be any more manic, but the darkness seems to sharpen the senses and make you notice it even more. Locals are sitting on little plastic stools (the type you'd use at home if you were a little on the short side and needed to get something out of a high cupboard) and necking the 'Bia Hoi' (piss-weak, local-brewed beer that costs a penny a glass), whilst mopeds whiz by. We visit a restaurant (much to the amazement of the locals) and try a couple of traditional Vietnamese dishes: some kind of steamed dumpling with a questionable filling and fried onions and a very tasty noodle soup with beef. We pull up a few of the aforementioned stools on a street corner (actually in the road) and have a few Bia Hoi's before retreating to a bar where I notice a drum set and ask if I can have a go (I like to think I can play). The bar owner is very apologetic and explains that he doesn't have any sticks. After telling him not to worry, he approaches the pool table, takes one of the cues from the group of people playing and returns twenty minutes later with a couple of homemade sticks. After all that, I feel that I have to put a show on.

The night continues with a trawl round the cities many bars and trying to shake off the unwanted companionship of a chubby, middle aged Irishman with a major anger-management problem (not a good thing to have in Hanoi).

I spend two days on a wooden junk boat out in the turquoise waters of Halong Bay, sunbathing, kayaking, sleeping under the stars and swimming with some mean looking jellyfish amongst the thousands of limestone peaks. On return to the mainland, we take lunch in Halong City where I'm informed that dogs, cats, mice and maggots all make for a fine meal in Vietnam – good to know. We head back to the bedlam of Hanoi's streets; I book a night train down to Hue (and so, worryingly, does the angry, Irish chap – let's call him Joe). The highlight of my evening is my drunken stumble back to the hostel where I am confronted by an enormous rat that has appeared from underneath a closed restaurant shutter (I remind myself not to eat there). My immediate reaction is to boot it as hard as I can, so that's what I do. Unfortunately, I've forgotten I'm wearing flip-flops, and I end up vomiting. I've just wellied a rat in my bare feet.

To Hue

I reluctantly leave my new gang in sweaty Hanoi early the next evening, heading to the train station for my trip southward to Hue. Some prolonged bartering over my chosen dinner of a baguette and a pack of 'Laughing Cow' soft cheese almost results in me missing the train. After jumping onboard just as the train pulls away, I discover that my compartment set up is six fold-down tables in a cupboard – known as a 'hard sleeper'. The six people crammed into the compact space are myself, two Vietnamese fellows on the top beds/tables fast asleep, a Swedish and an American chap and good old 'Angry Joe' from Hanoi (the hostel had helpfully purchased us tickets in the same compartment – I'm beginning to think I may have been stitched up). The train is brightly lit and loud, so sleep is not easy to come by. We share our treats amongst us which makes for a highly unusual evening meal of baguette with laughing cow, 'after eight' chocolates, Baileys and neat Scotch. As the night moves on, the alcohol makes me tired and I attempt to sleep on my hard bed, succeeding only in picking up a few new bruises.

I step into Hue at eight the next morning to a hoard of taxi drivers; I see 'Angry Joe' edging through the throng toward me, almost certainly looking to team up. I can think of nothing worse so throw a quick body swerve behind a car, choose the tallest driver (had to select one somehow) and ask him to take me to a 'cheap and cheerful' hotel. I'm shown to just that and, after waiting for the two female receptionists to finish giggling at me, I book a simple room, dump Clive and set out for a 'day in Hue' (its pronounced h-way, you see?).

Hoi An

I spend a day sightseeing in Hue and the reception girls are still giggling from the previous morning when I leave to catch my 'tourist bus' to Hoi An. The journey progresses exactly as I expect; a 'three hour' trip takes five hours. We make assorted stops at crappy restaurants and a random cave full of sculptures where people sprint out of shops to try to flog carvings and pestles & mortars (always room for one of those in a backpack). During this stop I run out for a quick toilet break and one of my fellow passengers roots through my bag and selectively raids a handful each of Thai baht, US dollars and Vietnamese dong – awfully thoughtful of them to leave me with a little for myself. When we eventually pull into Hoi An, the driver announces that he knows several fine hotels and that we can all stay on the bus and choose which one we want to stay in. I'm not having that and jump straight off with a couple of English lads. We walk to the nearest hotel where we find a triple room for next to nothing (it's missing a bathroom door – that's how you get to know people quickly...).

We take a stroll around the compact town and it's a lovely, cosy place. A quaint historic centre with a river running along its edge, it's filled with tailors, art shops and a sprinkling of bars and restaurants. We cross a Japanese bridge, but are told halfway across that we're not supposed to be on it if we don't have a 'tourist ticket' and have to find another way into the centre. As we find our bearings, we're constantly hassled by women wanting us to come into their tailor shops and be measured for suits and shirts. The thought of buying a suit hadn't really crossed my mind, but I think 'why not?', and when we come across a friendly place that seems to know what they're talking about, we spend a couple of hours chatting, looking at colours and patterns and being fitted for five suits and ten shirts between the three of us.

A 'suit fitting' celebration ensues and we discover that there are a lot of 'happy hours' to be had in Hoi An, the bars do close early but it's a nice, chilled kind of town and that's just fine by us. We play pool in an upstairs bar and are joined by a snappily (some may say camply) dressed Vietnamese chap in a sleeveless top, flecked trousers and shiny shoes. He fancies himself as something of a hustler – he's absolutely awful and loses every game he plays before making his excuses and leaving. At closing time, there is a bevy of moto guys waiting at the entrance to cart people off to a 'late club – out of town'. I can't be bothered with the hassle and head back to the room.

The next day is themed: 'Exercise and Culture day', I meet up with a couple of Aussie lads I'd met in Hanoi and we hire some absolutely battered mountain bikes. Mine is a beauty – no gears, no brakes and one of the pedals is hanging off. We cycle the four kilometres to Cua Dai Beach and leave our precious cycles in a guarded bike shed. The large beach is almost empty and with the three of us being part of only a few people there, we are constantly being pestered by vendors wanting to sell drinks and fruit. We discover that they won't come into the sea, so we stay in there as long as possible before being caught when we nip out for a breather and eventually buy some fresh pineapple just to ward off the other women. We're frazzling underneath the midday sun, so we cover up and head back to Hoi An, weaving our way around shop owners who step out into our paths trying to get us to buy something.

After a second suit fitting and discovering that my trousers are slightly tight around the crotch (which I quite like), the culture part of the day begins. We buy the tourist ticket for Hoi An old town that allows you to 'make your own culture menu' as it were (you pick three sites of interest from ten - or something like that). We visit an ancient house, a museum of history and culture, the Japanese bridge that I've already walked over several times and a handicraft workshop (hooray!). We take a lengthy break in a nearby bar to discuss our final option and plump for the Phuc Kien Assembly Hall (partly because of the humorous name and partly because it was recommended by my tailor), which is very ornate and has a fantastic dragon statue. The afternoon of culture is ended and we wind down with a meal and a few drinks by the river whilst watching a fabulous sunset. Given the option of a thirteen-hour overnight bus or a train journey the following day, I plump for the train and spend another evening in Hoi An taking advantage of the happy hours, posting my new, crotch-hugging clothes home to the UK and dodging men on bikes who still want to take me to 'late club – out of town'.

Nha Trang

The Aussie lads and I spend the ten-hour train journey South to Nha Trang living like babies: nap, eat, toilet, nap, watch some scenery, eat and nap. The only contact we have with a human is when the conductor enters the compartment, takes my mp3 player and listens to it for five minutes before signalling his appreciation and leaving without checking our tickets – the weirdo.

We arrive in Nha Trang, Vietnam's premier seaside resort. After a couple of days here it seems that there's not much to do apart from sit on the beach by day and get drunk by night (perhaps that's why it's Vietnam's premier seaside resort). We've frequented the same, posh seafront bar on consecutive nights and keep making the same mistake with the Vietnamese vodka (drinking it). The beachfront is notorious for pickpockets and thieving prostitutes when darkness falls, and it looks like one fellow has been caught red-handed as he sprints along the beach and, after being rugby tackled by a couple of the local constabulary, is given a rather severe beating.

Angry Joe returns

On our last evening, after a day out on a 'party boat', we have a tasty meal accompanied by a few cold beers and I find myself standing in the middle of the road at a busy junction, bartering with a woman over a packet of chewing gum. Just as I come to my senses and wonder what on earth I'm doing, it's too late, and five other women have surrounded me to start a 'chewing gum price war'. The rest of the evening is something of a blur; 'buckets' rear their ugly head again for the first time since the Ko Phang Ngan incident, these must have killed my last few cells of common sense as Vietnamese vodka is inexplicably sampled once again. Some of the folks we bumped into whilst out on the party boat earlier are far worse for wear than our group, which makes me feel a little better, and we somehow manage to welcome 'Angry Joe' into our ranks – where did he come from? We end up dancing in the posh beach bar into the early hours for the third night running until I have the tremendous idea to run fully clothed into the sea, where I'm shortly joined by the Aussies and a few English girls we were drinking with. Some skinny dipping soon ensues and, whilst we're acting like clowns in the sea, 'Angry Joe' is falling asleep back in the bar and having his camera stolen off the table, before waking up, walking home and also having his wallet relieved by one of the working girls on the beachfront. Surprisingly, all our belongings are intact when we emerge from the sea and we stumble home for a couple of hours sleep.

Mui Ne

I'm rudely awoken and still drunk when the phone rings in the morning. I've absolutely no idea where I am and it takes a good thirty seconds to piece together how I've found myself in this situation (the soaking wet, sandy jeans clinging to my legs are something of a clue). Once I'm compus mentus I answer the phone and am asked 1) why we're not ready for the bus and 2) when are we planning to pay our bill. We throw all our gear into bags (including the soaking wet clothes from last night), put on some clothes and trudge down to the bus in a severe state of disrepair.

Someone must have let slip to Angry Joe which bus we were on, as he's up and ready to join us to Mui Ne, I'm not keen on listening to his discontented ramblings, so I find a nice row of seats at the back of the bus with a blanket and a pillow and curl up for a sleep – until I'm moved on five minutes later by the driver who tells me it's his bed (who's driving the bloody bus then?). The bus takes forever to make the southward trip to Mui Ne, we'd have been better off walking (if we could walk) – six hours drag by and feel like several days, our hangovers have kicked in with a vengeance and the mood in the camp (especially as we'd somehow inherited Angry Joe) is at an all time low.

We finally make it to Mui Ne, an exceptionally long stretch of slim beach lined with resorts and a popular place for wind and kite surfing. The bus driver starts the 'I've got a good hotel for you' routine again but we escape with the excuse of 'needing some fresh air', grab our bags and try to find a good deal for ourselves; one hour of traipsing in and out of guesthouses along the lengthy stretch of tarmac beside the beach that seems to stretch forever in the lunchtime sun later, and we've had no luck. The Aussies finally find a pricey room in a posh resort and state that they 'can't go on with the search any longer', I'm torn between having to share a room with Angry Joe (I struggle with being in the same time zone as him), or paying way over what I can afford for a room. I decide that the budget is more important than my sanity and reluctantly agree to share a room with Joe.

The drained, lifeless group shuffles to the nearest café to try and put some energy into our decimated bodies with the first food and fluid of the day. After a meal, some fruit and as much water as our bodies will carry, we drag ourselves back to the resort where everyone crashes out for the rest of the day. I sit on the beach and watch one of the most amazing sunsets I've ever seen;

the sky looks like a silent fireworks display – truly awesome. Nha Trang has washed me out and as soon as my head hits the pillow I'm out for the count.

We've booked ourselves an old style army jeep for early the next morning and after a healthy, fruit breakfast I'm feeling rejuvenated. The jeep shows up with a driver, which is slightly disappointing as we were looking forward to driving ourselves. Four of us cram into the jeep, which is only designed for three additional passengers. We make for one of Mui Ne's major draws - the 'big red sand dunes' (not the official name). This collection of massive sand dunes sits just metres from the main road and, on pulling up to a shop opposite, we are immediately mobbed by a large group of excited local children who pull our clothes, ask our names, where we're from and whether we want to pay them some money to slide down the side of the big red sand dunes on a piece of plastic sheeting.

Trying to appreciate the dunes whilst being annoyed and poked is quite difficult; I make a run along the spine of one of the larger dunes in an attempt to create a bit of personal space but no sooner have I lined up a photo shot then the rabble of kids is around hassling me again. I manage to lose a few with another run but the group is still five or six strong and not letting up so, I give in and pay a cute little girl who was too small to annoy me to use her plastic sheet and ride the dune. It's not particularly exciting and the sand sticks to my sweaty/sun cream laden skin to form a thick red skin dough, making me look like a tall oompah-loompah.

We're driven to a nearby canyon, which is littered and covered in power cables and guided along the top by a local man who appears out of nowhere. Its sweaty work and, seeing the state of us on the way down, he shows us to a water tank that has numerous dead insects floating in it. We're all so hot, sweaty and sandy that we're not bothered and wash ourselves anyway. He requests payment and we chuck him a few thousand dongs to keep him happy.

Our last stop is a walk along the 'fairy stream' – a clear, shallow stream that comes up to the ankles and runs over the marbled red and white sand. As we set off (after gearing up with some walking sticks), we are met by two young lads who volunteer to guide us to the direction of a 'waterfall' for payment – it's pretty obvious which way we're supposed to be headed, so we reject their kind offer. After a kilometre walk, we arrive at the 'waterfall', which isn't as impressive as the scenery along the way but makes for a nice cool shower and a chance to wash off the remainder of the sand. As we jump back in the jeep and head back to the resort, the Aussie lads state that they're going to stay for another day – Angry Joe starts to ask questions about my itinerary and I tell him I'm probably going to stay as well, promptly booking onto a bus to Ho Chi Minh in an hours time.

Ho Chi Minh

My body is telling me that it's not ready for another bus ride in South-East Asia (especially my back), but I need to get away from Angry Joe, so there's no choice. As I wait for my bus, the man who sold me my ticket tells me of his love for England and asks whether I could employ him when I return. I tell him I have an opening for a personal assistant and will arrange an interview. The bus unsurprisingly shows up half an hour later than expected and is packed to the rafters; I manage to find a single seat but there's instantly a re-shuffle as an Asian couple and their pet monkey climb onboard and the driver wants to ensure they sit together, moving a few disgruntled backpackers. The trip that was alleged to be four hours was closer to six (equation for SE Asian bus trips – take time you're told and multiply by half again for an accurate journey time) and its night by the time we pull into Ho Chi Minh's budget accommodation hub – Pham Ngu Lao. I wearily climb from the bus and, as soon as my feet hit the floor of the pavement, a tiny woman grabs me and begins to drag me round guesthouses – despite the fact she's only a foot tall, I'm powerless to prevent this – I'm too tired. I just tell her to get me a room in a cheap, clean and friendly place and take the first one she finds. I dump Clive, check that my room is secured and go out to search for some dinner. I'm offered a 'motorbike sex massage' by one of the many moto fellows hanging around the streets, which sounds awfully strange – I decline his offer after lengthy consideration.

The hot and sticky streets here are as mad as those of Hanoi, so I decide to stop at a busy bar with wicker chairs on the pavement for a beer to gather my bearings. The madness pours from the streets, onto the pavements and into the bars – nowhere is safe! Within five minutes of taking my seat, seller after seller offers me photocopied guidebooks and cult novels, tiger balm, chewing gum, postcards, paintings and cigarettes. I'm mesmerised by the non-stop activity and before long, I've forgotten all about dinner and just sit people watching and drinking lovely, cold beer.

The next morning I awake drenched in sweat. My fan has cut off. The power must have gone during the night and has not returned. After a cold shower, I join a crowd of tourists spilling off the pavement outside; there are a couple of travel agents awaiting coaches to the Cu Chi tunnels. On boarding one of five buses out to the tunnel site, our guide (a rambling toothless fellow) hops on the microphone and tells us a little about the tunnels – there's so much echo on the mic that we can't understand a word he's saying. The tunnels are hopelessly touristy but interesting nevertheless. When it comes to crawling through the tiny underground tunnels (even though they've been made considerably larger for tourists), I find it a real, hot struggle. I don't think I would have excelled in the Viet Cong. We're taken to the loud and expensive shooting range; it all feels a little tacky so I just browse the attached gift shop and buy some water to replace the fluid I lost in the tunnels.

On the way back to the city, I'm dropped off the bus at the war remnants museum - which is pretty hardcore. There's a collection of photographs of the conflict taken by US photographers including some amazing images. There is also an exhibit on 'Agent Orange' – the mutilations caused by the US chemical weapons (including deformed foetus in jars which is upsetting) and details of massacres in villages along with some graphic photos. Obviously the information is one-sided, but you do come out with real feeling for the plight of the Vietnamese people.

I walk back to my 'neighbourhood' and the power is still out everywhere, so I return to my favourite wicker chair on the pavement and drink wonderfully cold beer until darkness falls and block by block the electricity visibly returns (apart from mine). I walk down to the next block and find the first restaurant with power, order some food and do a little writing. I notice a tourist bus dropping off outside and see a familiar face descending the steps – Angry Joe. I slide under the table and peer through the chairs opposite, he's dragged off swearing by one of the mad little ladies on the sidewalk and I breathe a sigh of relief. I return to my chair once again and wait for the barrage of sellers: I'm offered lighters (marijuana & cocaine), a confused moto guy offers me some 'Marajar', more photocopied books, roses, cigarettes and a tiara that flashes (I bought two of these). Angry Joe is obviously staying in the neighbourhood, and as he walks by, I hide behind a cocktail menu before returning to my hotel where the power has finally returned but the hot water hasn't.

The first person I see when I reach the bottom of the stairs the next morning is Angry Joe. As luck would have it, he's staying at my hotel, just two rooms away in fact. He greets me enthusiastically and offers a place at his table for breakfast; I just can't get my head round the idea of spending any more time in his company so, despite being hungry, I decide to skip breakfast and get something later. I tell him I've got to get to the bank before it shuts. That'll do nicely.

I spend an entire day bargain hunting in the markets and another with a lengthy, backside-numbing moto ride out onto the Mekong Delta (where the Mekong River meets the sea) before heading back to Ho Chi Minh. My last night in Vietnam is spent with the Aussie boys again, sitting in a restaurant with the locals, watching the national team take on Singapore at football; I've got one eye on the game and one eye on my noodle soup, as I'm unfamiliar with the look and texture of the meat floating in it. I gather some on a chopstick and show it to the chap next to me with a quizzical look – he grins and gives me the thumbs up – I think I'm eating dog.

23 – Cambodia

The Border

After all the bad press I've heard about the trouble with getting into Cambodia, I'm expecting a bureaucratic nightmare. I pass through the Vietnamese side with ease and stride down a dusty path toward Cambodia; it's baking hot and I'm being closely followed by flies. I walk past an impressive new border building that's springing up; it looks like its near completion. I begin to wonder if I'm about to stride straight into Cambodia unopposed when a shout comes from a tin hut across the way - that'll be the passport control then. I brace myself for an episode but the process is fast and smooth, no bribes or sign of the alleged corruption I'd been warned about. I fill out an arrival form, show my visa, have a chat about how the new border building is coming along and that's that.

I'm shown into a restaurant along the way and told that my onward bus will not be arriving for another three hours, this turns out to be a ruse, as an extremely compact minivan shows up less than an hour later and, after an immense struggle to fit eleven people and eleven bags inside, we're all packed in and ready to go. We reach a river and a ferry crossing point; the moment we pull to a halt the van is surrounded by people trying to sell goods or beg for money. Despite the heat, we have to close the windows, as that is the only way to stop people reaching in. The river is crossed and we bounce over the uneven roads, past endless fields and open space, to Phnom Penh.

Phnom Penh

Once again we're conveniently dropped into the reception of a guesthouse, but they've only got a tiny room on the roof with a mattress for me and I think I can probably do a little better than that. I find a cheap, yet clean & welcoming place on a dusty backstreet, which does the job. There's a little daylight left, so I take a short walk down to the independence monument and Sihanouk Boulevard where a grinning teenage lad on a motorbike asks whether he can take me anywhere. I tell him that the only place I'm headed is back home for a beer but he follows me home and is insistent that he drive me around the city tomorrow, explaining that he has no parents and a family to look after. Whether this is true or not, he looks young and desperate, so I tell him to show up the next morning. Whilst I'm sampling a bottle of 'Angkor' beer and a curry, the driver from the guesthouse introduces himself and starts negotiating a fee for driving me around tomorrow. I've just discovered that they can get hold of Beerlao in Phnom Penh and order a bottle straight away – I'll deal with this guy in the morning.

After a night's sleep largely interrupted by dogs fighting, the guesthouse's nominated driver is waiting for me when I open my room door. I explain that I've agreed to go with the lad (who's already waiting outside the front door smiling, god knows how long he's been there), because he's got a family to look after. The guesthouse driver pleads that he also has family to look after but I figure he probably gets more business through the guesthouse than the kid gets from pestering tourists on the street, so stick with my decision. The kid is overjoyed to see me and we barter (not very hard) for a price for the day, I tell him where I want to go and we're away.

My first port of call is 'S21', also known as Tuol Sleng – a schoolhouse that was converted into a prison by the Khmer Rouge, who took control of Cambodia after the Vietnam War. Led by the evil Pol Pot, their 'revolution' involved re-naming the country 'Democratic Kampuchea', re-locating everyone to work out in the countryside, abolishing education, religion and currency and imprisoning, torturing and murdering their own people. Vietnam invaded in 1978 and overthrew the evil regime which then led to widespread famine, killing hundreds of thousands more whilst civil war continued throughout the 1980's. An estimated two million people (including many of the educated adults) died during this time - an unfathomable 20% of the country's then population.

Tuol Sleng is a hard-hitting place, as it seems to have been left almost exactly how it was when the Khmer Rouge abandoned it. There are horrific pictures of murdered prisoners chained to beds (with the beds and manacles still present in the room you stand in) that make everything seem vivid, like you're in the middle of it. Some of the upstairs classrooms have been filled with harshly made brick cells and there is a collection of haunting photos of those that perished here. After watching a film telling the tale of a couple who were separated and killed during the revolution, I walk through an exhibition of former workers in the prison and members of the Khmer Rouge that were tracked down during an investigation to see where they were now. Finally I reach a heavily desecrated picture of Pol Pot, with the word 'cunt' scrawled on his forehead.

I breathe a deep sigh and run a gauntlet of beggars outside of the school, jump onto the moto and head out into the countryside and Choeung Ek – the killing fields. From 1975-1978, seventeen-thousand men, women and children were transported here from Tuol Sleng and executed. Most were bludgeoned to death to avoid wasting bullets. Nine thousand people's remains were exhumed from the mass graves in 1990 and the skulls now sit in a huge memorial stupa. Nowadays, it's just a peaceful meadow out in the countryside, full of craters.

After buying my moto dude and myself some lunch, I go and see the Royal Palace (wearing appropriate clothing this time and not having to borrow a pair of clowns trousers), which, although not dissimilar to the one in Bangkok, is far quieter. I was one of only ten people walking around. There's a silver pagoda with an Emerald Buddha here you know, you can take a seat on the carpet and do whatever it is you do when confronted with an Emerald Buddha.

We return to the guesthouse, where I thank the kid and pay for his service. The power goes out across my part of town and I spend the evening drinking beerlao for what may be the last time whilst reading by lantern, before retiring to my room to be kept awake by cats fighting - they must alternate fighting days with the dogs.

To Siem Reap

I'm up at six in the morning to catch my bus to Siem Reap - the gateway to the ancient temples of Angkor. The bus station in Phnom Penh is a melee of people and it takes me some time to fight through the crowds of sellers and climb onto my bus, I'm wearing a pair of sunglasses but a man carrying a board full of them is badgering me to buy some of his and will not leave me alone. I explain that I only possess one pair of eyes; perhaps he's better off targeting someone else? There's a strange seating policy: the driver looks you up and down and then decides where you're going to sit. Unfortunately, I'm seated next to a strange, French chap in a vest and a pair of red cycling shorts sporting a bum bag. He's dancing along to a Cambodian music video playing on the TV at the front of the bus and looking around to see who thinks he's a hilarious man. No one is looking. He continues for three or four minutes and then finally realises he looks like a prize idiot (even without the dancing) and takes his seat. The bus is full to capacity but locals are still clambering aboard. The solution to this is to fill the aisle with little plastic stools for them to sit on − I imagine what will happen if we brake suddenly and have a little chuckle. An old lady next to me breaks into a shrill laugh which is akin to a power drill in ones temple.

Six hours of head-splitting laughter later, we arrive at the concrete bus station in Siem Reap and are greeted with a near riot. The best part of thirty men are clambering for position by the door of the bus, holding signs and getting ready to pounce on the tourists. The local police are making a token effort to keep them in line, but are being overwhelmed. As people step off the bus, all hell breaks loose and things start to get messy. I'm surrounded by five men who are all grabbing me and trying to get me into their rickshaws to town; I'm trying to remain calm but they won't take their hands off me so I struggle free. A smartish looking chap who speaks some English offers to take me to my pre-booked guesthouse for a set price, so I jump into his cab just to get away from the melee and we set off. As soon as we're far enough away from the station, but not close enough to town, he stops and tells me that if I don't want to go to his guesthouse of choice then the fare will quadruple − I pick up Clive, jump out and tell him where he can go.

Siem Reap

As I walk toward my guesthouse, a couple more moto drivers stop and try to sell me their services; all I want to do is get to my accommodation and, finally, a man offers to drive me there with no strings attached. That is until we get to the guesthouse where he outlines his availability for three-day tours – I explain that I'm planning on getting some exercise and hiring a mountain bike (showing him my ever increasing fat deposits). After twenty minutes, he finally gets the message. My chosen guesthouse is absolutely deserted; I'm the only person staying here. As much as I'm comfortable in my own company, it would have been nice to have a few more people around. They have a 'communal house bike', which is a real rust bucket from many moons ago. I jump on and go to investigate the town.

Siem Reap is the nearest town to the temples of Angkor (and apparently home to Cambodia's only ATM). It is essentially a tourist town with all markets of accommodation from budget hostels to expensive hotels – catering for the huge crowds that flock to see the ancient temples. There are plenty of eateries, markets and Internet cafes and not a lot else. As I'm cycling down the main thoroughfare, the chain falls off my bike and I'm pedaling thin air. Showing anger is not the done thing in Asia, so I laugh and aim a swift kick at the back wheel. As I'm cursing my rotten luck, a tuc-tuc driver stops beside me, plays with the bike and, hey, presto! - it's cured. I thank the miracle worker, turn down his kind offer of a three-day tour of the temples and wobble my way back to my guesthouse.

I break the news to my fabulously friendly hostel owner that I'm only going to be staying for one night, as I want to stay somewhere with people. He offers me a lift back into town and I feel terribly guilty. I walk to a restaurant and am asked for money by several beggars, one follows me to the door and takes a piss on the street whilst I'm ordering, which is nice.

On my way home, I'm invited to join in a game involving a giant shuttlecock which is kicked into the air and kept up for as long as possible by the participating players. I impress the locals with my keepy-uppy skills and am offered some wine/petrol in return.

It burns a hole in my throat. I thank them with a croak and leave.

I'm on a mission the next day; I need to find a bike that actually functions and a guesthouse with people in. This doesn't take long, as I'm loaned a relatively new mountain bike for three days with absolutely no paperwork by a very trusting woman who also recommends a popular guesthouse a little nearer to the centre of town. I can now get on with why I really came here – the temples. I stock up on water and sunblock and set off on the dusty road toward the ancient city (at least I thought it was the road to the ancient city). I stop for help and adopt my 'lost face' and, with some more accurate directions, I'm on my way to the ticket centre. For a three-day pass to the site, a passport photo is required and this is all arranged at the ticket office. It briefly dawns on me that I've never had an attractive passport photo (this may be because I'm unattractive). The pass is 40 US dollars, which I could probably live for a month on here but I'm ready to make the most of it.

I decide to start with the main attraction - 'Angkor Wat'. I've seen photos and models but was not ready for the sheer size of the place when I pulled up beside it. There is a lot of reconstruction work taking place, so it's not quite as I imagined, but still very striking. The complex is immense; you could probably spend three days in just these grounds and not see everything. I wander the main temple and check out the amazing architecture and the huge, intricate 'reliefs' that stretch around the building. People are sitting around the grounds taking in the aura of the place, some having a sleep (not a bad idea) and others just finding a little spot up on one of the ancient buildings, marveling and trying to imagine what would have happened here. The huge grounds are being well worked by an army of gardeners.

On exiting the temple grounds and collecting my bike, I'm rushed by a group of children attempting to pull me into their family's food/souvenir tents outside. I order some soup and spend the next half an hour answering questions from various children and turning down the opportunity to purchase postcards. My next temple is a hill climb away; I've actually worn sensible footwear for once and am quite glad, as there are a few snakes around. This temple, Phnom Bakheng has a distant view of Angkor Wat and the surrounding countryside. I then cycle toward 'The Bayon', a temple with many huge, carved faces staring out – a spooky place. The sun is sinking so I pass by Angkor Wat to see if there's an opportunity for a nice, sunset moment but there's nothing doing. A group of local children cycle up and ask me seventy questions about not much in particular, but they're nice kids (and aren't selling anything) so I go along with the quiz. I pause for a sit by a lake on the way home for a short while, but the combination of mosquito repellent, sun cream, dirt and sweat has left my skin heavily caked and I'm feeling horrible, so I return to my new guesthouse in Siem Reap. My much-needed shower floods my room and soaks my belongings. Nice one.

A fantastic fish curry and a couple of cold beers soon improve my mood and I have a few games of pool at a bar with some backpackers before being offered some 'massage, lady, boom-boom' by the moto driver taking me home – I'm not sure about this combination, so opt for a sleep instead.

Another day of 'templing' begins. I flood my room again (I'd been told the problem had been fixed), have a huge breakfast and with a slightly bruised bottom (from yesterdays cycling rather than the massage, lady, boom-boom) I set off on the road back to Angkor. I pass Angkor Wat and start at one of a long list of temples to get round today, Ta Prohm – the famous temple with the huge tree trunks bursting through its crumbling ruins. After a couple more temples I begin to lose track of which is which and need a break to get my head straight. I exit whichever temple I happen to be in at the time and am mobbed by vendors steaming out of their stalls toward me "Sir! Cold drink? Something to eat? T-shirt? Postcard?"

I settle for a cold drink and six t-shirts and am instantly surrounded by children selling postcards (and mini Hindu gods) again. This becomes too much for me and I jump back on the bike, deciding to visit some of the temples way out of the normal tourist radar. There is only me and a photographer in one of the places I visit, it's so quiet. I pause for another cold drink outside and am taken in by a friendly family running the food stall; they're great company and we talk for ages. I somehow inherit a mother, sister and a wife (my second of the trip) in the process. I cycle through a village and past paddy fields, way out into the countryside, until I reach my last temple of the day – Banteay Samre. I attempt to impress a group of children gathered at the corner selling postcards by steaming through a large puddle, unfortunately it's a tad deeper than I anticipate and I plunge into a lake and become stuck before falling off into the muddy depths. They all dance with joy and I become a captive audience for their postcard selling. I feel a touch sheepish.

It's getting dark, what time is it? Where am I? I impress the locals (and regain some of my street cred) as I pass back through the village with a fine display of non-handed cycling. It's a fair old way back to Siem Reap and there's no way I'm going to make it before sundown. There's utter carnage at Phnom Bakheng, as every tourist in town (apart from me) had gathered for an 'intimate' sunset (between a few hundred people) and they now pour down the hillside together. I get caught up in the traffic returning to town as I weave in between the rickshaws and buses, taking on a few lungfulls of exhaust fumes. I finally make it back to the guesthouse, dizzy and with a raw throat. I must have cycled more than thirty kilometres today; my whole body aches and I've got some serious saddle sores. A magnificent cold beer and a welcome icy shower (this time without flooding my room) get me back on track. I have dinner in town, ensuring I have a pad and pen with me - this gives the impression you're a food critic and you receive larger portions.

Sunrise

My alarm sounds at a mind-numbing 4.44am – sunrise at Angkor Wat is a must-do on a visit to Cambodia. I stagger tiredly from my room, reluctantly mount my bike, feel all the bruises on my rear awakening and begin to negotiate the dark streets. That is until I hear a nasty noise and realise that I've got a flat tyre – you couldn't make it up! A crowd of taxi drivers instantly swarm around me as they sense a good fare, but I reject their advances and continue the journey with the vague hope that there's a chap with a pump out on the street at five in the morning – amazingly there is – I imagined it and it came true (can't think of how many times that hasn't worked). Now with air in my tyres, I cycle out of Siem Reap toward Angkor once more. At least I think I'm heading toward there: it's absolutely pitch black and the only time I can see where I'm going is when a moto/tuc-tuc/bus passes and I can pick up the road from their headlights.

Angkor Wat is still in darkness but there's a steady stream of tourists and torches walking (the torches aren't walking) into the temple and trying to find their own space for the sunrise. I walk out across the grounds away from the crowds and lean up against a pillar; I don't have my own space for long and am soon joined by a couple of photographers. The sunrise is unfortunately a bit of an anticlimax, as it turns out to be a heavily cloudy morning and the hoards leave disappointed. I temple onwards, walking along the 'Terrace of the Elephants' and visiting the grounds behind it. I realise it's nine in the morning and I haven't eaten, so I cycle past a group of food stalls and am rushed by a lady. I don't have the energy to carry on and let her guide me into her stall and plonk me on a chair. On stopping, I realise just how tired I am and how much my body aches. I can't go on, finish my breakfast and cycle very slowly back to Siem Reap for some sleep.

A tuc-tuc driver I bumped into earlier has waited patiently for an hour outside my guesthouse whilst I pack and have my last meal. We set off for the airport in Siem Reap and I marvel for one last time at the madness of Cambodia's and South East Asia's streets – people on the move everywhere you look and so much going on...

Siem Reap airport is a tiny, nearly-new terminal; jam-packed full with far too many passengers for its petite size. Check in is an absolute mess and takes forever - there are fourteen desks crammed into enough space for three. The area is a throng of tourists, and a Japanese tour group has just caused mayhem by shoving their way to the front of the huge queues. A Swiss woman has trod on my toe three times, I decide that a fourth will result in my drop-kicking her across the terminal.

The 'departure tax' from Cambodia is an unprecedented 25 US dollars; I see a sign proclaiming the opening of a new terminal in the near future – I think I've just paid for the catering outlets. My flight to Bangkok is delayed and I'm offered a free meal voucher for the 'Angkor Grand Lounge' (or something along those lines) – by the time I make my way up to this lounge, most of the food has already been consumed by the other compensated passengers so I make do with a pile of meat and some cold rice and stay as long as I can in the comfortable surroundings before I have to go back to the stress of the waiting area.

I stop over for a night in Bangkok and then have to part with my third Thai departure tax of the trip on leaving; cursing when it occurs to me just how much Chang beer I could have bought with that lot. Early the next morning, I take my connecting flight to Singapore, and am thoroughly entertained by my Chinese co-passengers - as soon as the seatbelt light goes off on landing, they all immediately leap from their seats in unison and see who can get their belongings first. I've got a lengthy wait for my onward flight so sit tight until the fuss dies down and walk off last.

As an aside, Singapore airport is fantastic; a wonderful place to be stuck in – free internet terminals, a library (book store), sports TV (sitting on a ledge near a bar and watching goal highlights), drinks (water fountain) and an art gallery (photo competition) – this makes it very easy to waste five hours without spending a penny of my ever decreasing funds. For once, I'm praying there's a delay to my next flight as I'm due to arrive into Perth, Australia at 1am. Unfortunately everything goes to plan and I land in Perth - bang on time. Time to find somewhere to sleep...

24 – Australia

Skint in Oz

Even after dragging my heels at immigration and customs I still find myself standing in the arrivals area at two in the morning. There's no public transport for another four hours and there's no way I can afford a taxi so I need to find somewhere to get my head down. I ask a security guard if he can recommend a decent spot and he reels off the best ones, Perth airport isn't very large so they're easy to locate. Unfortunately I'm a bit late and all the comfiest benches have long been taken and are housing sleeping people. All I can find is a padded bench in one of the fast food restaurants and try to make myself comfortable on there. There is a loud, recorded tannoy announcement every twenty minutes that drowns out even my music and this continues for the entire night. I'll drift off into a light sleep and jump awake minutes later when the announcement belts out. When the restaurant staff arrives at 5.30am and start bashing around, I give up and wait for the first shuttle buses to Perth to start running. I select a backpackers hostel at random (there are always plenty to choose from in Oz), and am dropped off at the entrance. I just about have the energy to check in and fall into bed.

On my first full day in Australia, it becomes apparent that the cost of living has risen since my last visit and it's going to be a monumental struggle to get by on my budget. My plans needed to be drastically altered so after a couple of days in Perth, and some time down in the wine region of Margaret River (I can highly recommend jumping on a mountain bike and touring the vineyards for some free wine tasting), I hot tail it across to Adelaide before seeking refuge at a friends place in Melbourne to save on accommodation costs. I spend some time catching up with my brother who's working and living in the city and only move on to Sydney once it's almost time to leave Australia.

Sydney – A day on memory lane

The thirteen-hour coach trip from Melbourne to Sydney (in a silver bullet) lasts forever. I'm unable to sleep and spend most of the journey trying to figure out how a massive woman across the way is managing to fit her sizeable bulk across two seats and have a comfortable sleep - I'm quite jealous. We make a 'meal stop' at a truckers café but there's little more than pie and chips on offer and I don't feel like that at all. After a brief stop at Canberra to pick up some more passengers (one of whom sits next to the big lass and ruins her bed), we arrive into Sydney at eight in the morning and it's buzzing with commuters. I've chosen a central backpackers hostel in the city, as I'm only here for one night; my hostel is a short walk across Alfred Park. I check in, secure Clive and head off for some much-needed breakfast at a nearby cafe. My bacon and egg roll and hot sweet tea is made a little less enjoyable by a chain-smoking old woman named Mary and an extremely smelly fellow who I name 'BO-and-piss guy', which is fairly accurate judging by the stains on his clothing.

I have twenty-four hours to re-acquaint myself with the city that I spent a large chunk of my 'year out' in (having said that, I do take a year out every alternate year). I walk past old workplaces and bars I once frequented down to Circular Quay, pause for another marvel at the Opera House, sitting under a picture perfect, cloudless, deep-blue sky. I walk through the Botanic Gardens, recalling a wondrous New Year's Eve past. Last time I was here, these gardens were packed with revellers – now there are masses of lunch hour joggers in all shapes and sizes. I walk through The Rocks, pausing (and smelling) at restaurants that I'd love to be able to afford to eat in someday. I take my old bus out to Coogee Bay, the beach suburb I lived in and probably one of the biggest backpacker hot beds in the city, passing the 'rainbow walk' along Oxford Street with it's gay bars that unassuming backpackers sometimes unwittingly stride into (that would be me).

We pull up beside my old favourite local and one of the finest pubs in the world – The Coogee Bay Hotel. I would often (well, every day) step off the bus after a hard days work and stroll straight into the pub for a nice, cold beer. I have business with a certain, old favourite pie shop to attend to, almost having a heart attack when I find that it's not there but I've got my bearings slightly wrong and find it further up the street. I order my regular pie and take it down to the beach. I realise that I've neglected to pick up a fork and struggle through my pie, mash, mushy peas and gravy (strange choice for a baking hot summer's day I know) with my fingers and a lid. I survey the crowds of backpackers skiving work and expect to bump into someone I know but everyone is long gone; they're all back at their desks in the UK probably wishing they were still here. I can't hold off the lure of the pub any longer and trudge up to the Coogee Bay Hotel, sup on an ice-cold beer and all the memories come flooding back. It all feels a little lonely now without the old faces, and I bid farewell to Coogee, my pie shop, the pub and the beach and head back to my hostel in the city.

I'm up at six-thirty in the morning to catch a shuttle bus to the airport, my driver looks as unhappy as me to be up at such a time and doesn't say a word for the entire journey - can't say I mind. I check in and walk through the blinding lights of the duty-free lounge before boarding my flight to New Zealand. High winds play havoc with the flight, we're pretty much blown all the way to New Zealand; the lovely child behind me kicks the back of my seat for the entire journey, until a large drop in altitude sends a couple of kids into tears which starts a domino effect, as all the children on board begin to cry. Everyone is concerned about the landing (especially when we seem to be falling into the sea at one point), but all is well when a runway appears and we touch down safely at Auckland airport.

25 – New Zealand

There's a small issue with my short stay in New Zealand. I spent my time in Paihia, up North in the Bay of Islands, meeting a fantastic crowd of people at my hostel and spending the entire time doing not much other than drinking and laughing (there was a catamaran ride but it's all a bit of a blur). So, unfortunately, there's not a lot I can recount to you. However, if you don't mind, I would like to recount a tale told to me whilst I was there, and a similarly entertaining one from my last visit to the country a few years before:

The Amazing Maori (as told by James)

I met some hilarious Maori chaps in Paihia on the day of my arrival. They were staying at the same hostel we were; there were three of them and they were the first people I bumped into when I checked into the hostel. It was the early afternoon and they were already fairly drunk. Two of them (they were brothers if I recall correctly) had just picked up the third from jail that very day. He had been in for eight months or so on a drunk driving charge. I sat with them at a picnic table for the entire afternoon drinking beer and listening to their 'stories'. Well, more accurately, listening to a non-stop stream of hilarious lies. Below is a rough list of some of the things that were claimed that afternoon, with absolutely no exaggeration:

1) I once worked on a ranch and used to tame wild stallions then ride them bareback. The stallions were so enormous that if they kicked out their back legs they would hit those drainage pipes behind you (the pipes were around ten feet in the air).

2) I have seen people front-flip and back-flip stallions (we're presumably still talking about the ten-foot high ones).

3) My friend got shot with a shotgun blast in his chest. I reached into his chest and grabbed onto his lung to squeeze off the blood flow so that he wouldn't bleed to death. Then I made a

traditional poultice out of bark and leaves and packed the wound with it. He was better and walking around within a few days.

4) I went to South Central in L.A. and got in a fight with a gang. The leader of the gang stepped up to me and pointed his gun in my face, but I snatched the gun out of his hand and turned it on him. After that I gained the gangs respect.

You couldn't make it up. Or rather you could.

The Stalker (as experienced by me)

I toured New Zealand in early 2003 on one of those 'young persons' coach tours. There was a Brazilian girl on my trip, and I realised early on that she seemed to have taken a rather unhealthy interest in me. Unfortunately, although she wasn't altogether bad looking, she was what can only be described as 'stark, raving bonkers'.

After I'd made her acquaintance during an evening game of cards and noticed her staring at me intensely a couple of times, the whole sorry episode began in earnest. Basic intrusions into my aura, uncomfortable closeness to my face during conversations, constantly sitting next to me during meals and on the coach and removing my CD player (hey, this was way before mp3) headphones during coach journeys to ask me personal questions. I mean, this just isn't the behaviour of someone balanced. So anyway, I adopt my age-old (and consistently proven) tactic of ignoring and generally sneering in her general direction, which 99% of the time deflects unwanted attention in a matter of seconds. Unfortunately, this happens to be the other 1%. My Brazilian friend just figures I'm playing hard to get and takes this as a clear sign that I'm 'there for the taking' before upping the stakes. Cue her saving me a seat next to her on the bus and refusing to let anyone else sit there, asking me which aftershave I wear so she can buy some for herself (Hai Karate, I reply through a suppressed smile) and offering me CD's from her collection as gifts. She even pays to do a bungee jump with me, even though it's obvious when we arrive that she's absolutely petrified of heights and can't go through with it. Madness.

So, after touring the North and South islands of New Zealand, the bus drops off back in Christchurch a couple of weeks later and yours truly has a plan. My Latino friend queries my choice of backpackers and, cunningly, I tell her that I'm staying in the one across town, when in reality I'm staying in one slap bang on the square. You're all thinking 'genius', right? Wrong. She books into the other one and, then realising that her choice of murderous obsession isn't there, begins on a citywide hunt for the backpackers I'm staying in. This is all unbeknown to me of course and as I stride whistling happily into my hostel reception after a grand days sight seeing - lo and behold! - 'Bunny boiler April 2003' has had a fruitful days detective work and after locating my whereabouts is attempting to book a bunk in my room for the next three nights.

She somehow manages to get a bed in the dorm next door as mine is full, and tries her utmost to find out the time of my onward flight to Auckland (after that I'll imagine she'll be in my room in Auckland when I arrive before stowing herself away in my luggage for my onward flight to L.A). I tell her I'm going to see a film and she tags along (there was an attempt at hand-holding which I managed to avoid). Things take an interesting turn at this juncture, as I'm running extremely low on cash and she spies an opening; she invites me out for a meal and drinks on her (not ON her, she's paying). Now, this may not be a wise or gentlemanly thing to do (I know I'm going to become unpopular here), but as I was dreading toast and water for dinner I accept. I choose an eatery and she sits and stares at me for an hour whilst I eat and she has nothing. We then return to the hostel bar where she plies me with beer after beer. I should be able to see what's coming, but the more I drink, the more relaxed and blasé I become. It isn't until she's leading me by hand to her room (and possible death) that I suddenly come to my senses and begin to pull away with a look of sheer terror in my eyes. She grabs hold of my buttocks whilst I'm still within touching distance, wrenches me toward her and thrusts her tongue into my mouth. I can't breathe and feel like she's swallowing my face. When she eventually surfaces for air after some minutes, I run like the wind and hide in the nearest open room. After a little cry, I convince someone to go on a scouting mission to see whether she's walking the corridors; I'm given the all clear and quickly dive into my room. I'm too scared to come out again until the morning when I sprint with my backpack out of the hostel, worried she may be following me.

I'm sure that one day she'll track me down, and next time I won't be so lucky.

26 – Argentina

After flying from Auckland to Santiago, I spend a night in the Chilean capital. I'm not staying on in Chile, as I want to make it across to Argentina and Buenos Aires in time for the New Year celebrations, spending Christmas somewhere in between. I take a bus out early the following morning, negotiating a visually stunning route through the snow tipped mountains and thrashing rivers of the Andes, eventually arriving at the Argentinean border and the incredibly slow (and cold) immigration process that greets you.

Mendoza

The moment we finish the lengthy customs check and step back on the warm bus, I fall into a deep sleep, not waking until we're pulling into the pleasantly warm city of Mendoza. It's a busy bus station, the junction for many onward journeys, and I grab a taxi to my hostel after arranging to meet two bubbly Canadian sisters, and an Aussie chap whom I met on the bus, for drinks later. The cabbie points out various sights along the way, but my grasp of Spanish is exceptionally poor (which will make for many interesting situations) and I just smile and reply 'si' an awful lot (perhaps more than is necessary). My first comedy exchange comes moments after settling into the hostel, when I walk to a nearby launderette with Clive's entire contents and try to arrange for a next day collection, suddenly realising that I don't know any of the words I require apart from 'mañana' – I use this and some of my tried and tested hand signals to communicate my needs to the lady behind the desk – we'll see what happens.

Mendoza is still lovely and warm at seven in the evening and I meet my bus buddies at a Plaza in between our two hostels, 'Plaza Independecia' is a hive of activity; couples and groups are sitting at benches and on walls beside the large fountain and buzzing around various market stalls. We're the only ones up and about at 8pm, and find that the city (and country) doesn't really get going until the late hours. We find a bar that's thinking about opening up and convince them by helping to lay out the tables so we have somewhere to sit and drink a few cold beers whilst watching an assortment of battered old vehicles pull up at the junction and stall. This becomes a game where you guess which rust bucket will become the next to stall at the junction. As it passes ten in the evening, the restaurants begin to open for trade and we find a posh looking but cheap (fortunately, most things in Argentina are cheap) restaurant to try some of the fantastic Argentinean steak that backpackers passing me in the opposite direction have raved about. An hour later, after a huge, tasty steak in a warm, relaxed atmosphere for what turned out to be £4, all I'm ready for is a nice snooze. All before the locals have even come out to play.

I've arranged to move hostels, to the place my newfound friends are staying in, this morning and am attempting to holler a cab. They are all either occupied or ignoring me, so I try moving to a busier street with the same success. A taxi finally stops a little further down the street and I haul Clive over to the car before he screeches off laughing just as I reach him. After half an hour of this, I end up returning to my hostel and asking them to book me a car, which arrives in two minutes flat.

My new hostel appears to be in an area of the city that is heavily frequented by 'ladies of the night' (and day) – not an unusual occurrence for a backpackers. After becoming acquainted with Spanish speaking supermarkets and desperately trying to remember Spanish words for foodstuffs, I join a group from the hostel on a wine tour.

We pile into a minibus filled with fellow backpackers and a few holidaymakers (obviously on a tight budget if they've chosen the same tour as us!), and drive to the first *bodega* (wine shop). We are met by a face-slappingly beautiful woman (something Argentina has more than it's fair share of) who proceeds to talk us through some of the regions wines in flawless English, whilst showing us the winery and what is entailed in making the wine. She then pours us all an ample serving of several local red wines. I fall in love; she doesn't look at me twice (which obviously means she's a little stuck up).

Our second port-of-call is a little more traditional, containing big concrete pools and huge wooden casks, including one that apparently holds nine-thousand litres of wine — we consider tucking in between us. At the final vineyard we are given a master class in wine tasting, involving the swilling, smelling and tasting techniques. We are then treated to a meal of salami, cheese, bread and pickles washed down with plenty of red wine — not a bad way to spend an afternoon.

The gap between the evening and when the city comes to life is filled with some traditional drinking games - until we are told of a 'discotheque'. Even arriving at one in the morning the party is not quite underway, so we pay a sizeable cover to enter the establishment and it's more like a cabaret club where everyone is sat at tables chatting. A band emerges and breaks into a Spanish rendition of Robbie Williams 'Angels' which gets a few of the local girls (and consequently, me) excited, and by the time they've moved onto the more upbeat numbers there are packets of women up and dancing throughout. A DJ comes on and the staff begins to clear the tables and chairs; it's four in the morning and the night is just beginning for the locals, unfortunately we've peaked a little too early again and can no longer stand, let alone impress with our Latino dancing techniques. We take a taxi back to the hostel, impressing the driver with our stunning grasp of the language.

I awake the next morning with what I think is the worst headache I have ever had: It's like someone is putting a power drill to my temples. When I open my eyes and hear drilling, I begin to question what is going on and find that a well-needed air conditioning unit is being installed above my head. Several attempts at blocking out the din and getting some well needed sleep fail and I drag my tired body downstairs only three hours after arriving back from my night out.

Christmas in Mendoza

It's Christmas Eve apparently; that certainly snuck up. Some croissants and a couple of mugs of strong black coffee bring me back to some sort of normality (I'm walking with my eyes open). I walk through the Plaza Indepencia, it's very quiet and the fountains are off. My grasp of Spanish numbers is definitely improving: I'm beginning to understand what I'm paying and what change I'm supposed to receive. After a couple of hours I'm seriously flagging, the air-con installation has finished and the dorm room is lovely and cool. I lay my head down for a snooze and don't awake until the evening. By the time I shower and head down to the common room, the food for the traditional Argentinean Christmas Eve celebrations is being shipped in; there's absolutely tons of the stuff.

We get set for the meal at nine in the evening (early by Argentinean standards) and sit down to a speech from the jolly owner of the hostel, who explains that we (the residents) are part of their family and the meal has been made with love for us – that's a sentiment you don't often find when you're backpacking! The food is amazing, bright and colourful with lots of cold meats, salads, stuffed tomatoes and many other bright dishes I've never seen. We all eat until we're bursting, which is apparently the cue for dessert. The champagne is then brought out with another toast from our wonderful host – Christmas Eve couldn't have worked out better.

Mendoza goes wild after we shout the countdown to midnight, the whole city pours out into the streets and there is a cacophony of noise as fireworks explode everywhere. People are throwing them into the street from doorways and windows and the tops of buildings, for half an hour it's like a war zone. A few air bombs signal the end of the explosions and we retreat back inside for more drinks and an impromptu sing along when a guitar is brought out, we're still singing when the sun comes up.

Christmas Day is as 'traditionally festive', as I've felt on my travels; I wake up with a decent hangover, slump down in front of the TV and watch a 'Harry Potter' movie, whilst the Canadian girls are fixing up as traditional a Christmas dinner as they can muster from the local ingredients. They certainly come good and put on a fantastic spread: cold meats, creamed corn, green beans, mash, butternut squash and carrots – washed down with plenty of Argentinean wine. We go out to a street lined with bars after midnight for a few al-fresco drinks; a local chap overhears us speaking in English and makes a point of bringing my attention to his t-shirt with the Falklands islands and a burning union jack.

The problem of going to bed at six in the morning is that the checkout times don't change. On the day of our departure to Buenos Aires, we still have to be out by eleven so the group drag themselves out of bed blurry eyed, then, all attempt to pack in a crowded dorm room, which results in several elbow related injuries. We stash the bags in storage before heading off to a park for a nap in the warmth under a shaded tree.

Losing a dear friend

We're carried back to the Mendoza bus station in a rickety old cab whose boot keeps flipping open throughout the journey. A plush-looking coach pulls into one of the many docking bays and we queue up to place our baggage in the hold. A gruff, dirty porter loads our bags and eyes me suspiciously. I give him a small tip to see if it might force anything close to a smile but it doesn't.

A comfortable overnight bus journey passes, but I still haven't managed to get a decent nights sleep traveling on a bus despite the luxury and comforts of those in South America (big comfy, reclining seats, movies and attendants on hand to serve drinks and snacks). My sleep deprivation does however allow me to have a private viewing of the spectacular sunrise whilst the rest of the coach is fast asleep, and not long after we pull into Buenos Aires.

We disembark and immediately identify and grab each other's bags and make sure everyone has all their gear. After the inspection, there's just one thing missing – Clive. I've passed out all the gang's bags but am now faced with an empty luggage hold. Clive is absolutely nowhere to be seen! I'm in panic, and don't know what to do next. We rush straight to the bus companies office to explain the situation (one of the Canadian girls speaks Spanish whilst I shake my fist at the office window) but they're not interested at all and just offer a couple of minutes worth of shrugging and no help. I telephone the hostel we're booked at hoping for some advice and they helpfully give me the number of the tourist police who arrange to meet me at the bus station police office an hour later.

When the English speaking (thankfully) police officer arrives, he advises me that it's more than likely that the bag (he's not comfortable calling it Clive) was probably taken off the coach at Mendoza just after we got on and that it's unlikely to be seen again. He explains that I should have been given a receipt and from now onward (now I have no belongings to stow), ensure that I always have a ticket for my bag. He then types up a letter and gives me a crime number and that's the end of that. I've lost my faithful servant Clive and I'm now in South America with nothing but the clothes on my back, my passport, camera and credit card (thank God I kept them in my pockets!).

New Year in Buenos Aires

After several frustrating days trying to organise an insurance claim in the UK by phone and fax, whilst trying to gather together enough belongings for the last leg of the trip (with the minimal cash and credit I have left), I decide it's high time to get into Buenos Aires life. I learn to walk with my head down so I can dodge the dog shit, take tango lessons (and utilize them badly) at a tango club and carry on the habit of eating plenty of red meat and drinking until the sun comes up. The hostel I'm staying at sums the city up, it's insanely busy, fun, dirty and never sleeps. Our cramped all-male dorm room is an absolute pit with one shower and a toilet between eight of us. I enter the bathroom one night to find a couple 'at it' on the floor. The fellow asks if I can come back later and I inform him that I certainly can if he doesn't mind me pissing on his bed. They retire into the shower cubicle.

On New Years Eve, I charge my batteries by following everyone else's lead and sleep in until four in the afternoon. For the evening, we've booked an al-fresco table at a rather posh restaurant in the San Telmo area of the city. The surroundings are perfect: a huge table for over twenty backpackers in a large cobbled square. Music and salsa dancing are laid on and the food is considerably richer than a backpacker would normally indulge in. The wine is flowing and the New Year is welcomed in several times for various European countries before it's our turn. Fireworks erupt, locals and gringos* embrace and champagne corks are flying, a bill is put together, the cash collected doesn't come near (that's a group of backpackers for you!) and once this is resolved, it's time to stagger to the pre-arranged club.

We become quite lost when it transpires that none of the group actually knows where this club is. I'm warned by the police for walking in the middle of the road clutching a glass of champagne – quite right too. We finally locate the club at two in the morning and it's yet to open. We join the crowds at the front of the queue with a knowing nod and, when the doors open, stroll straight in. I explore the huge, swanky place and, whilst I'm admiring the garden area, a chap outside shouts over the wall, asking me to help him smuggle some wine in. I'm too drunk to know right from wrong and help him out which wins me a bottle of wine as a reward. Someone falls into one of the decorative water pools outside and, whilst the onlookers are laughing, I strike up a conversation with a stunning Argentinean girl. Her limited English and my limited Spanish mean that it's a fairly sketchy conversation but we're getting on well and there is a definite chemistry between us. She moves a little closer and I realise that I'm about to start a new year with this beautiful girl – what luck! Suddenly, an angry looking fellow appears from inside and stomps towards me, waving his hands furiously and shouting at me in Spanish. It appears I've spent the last half an hour romancing his girlfriend. After apologizing profusely and having a little cry, I watch the New Year sunrise over Buenos Aries with a couple of friends – it's nice enough but not quite what I was expecting.

*Gringo

Someone who isn't Central American, a tourist, notably a backpacker is commonly known as a gringo. I've been told it's a non-offensive term, but have been in situations where I'm not convinced. The more 'gringo-esqe' traits you display (poor command of the language, dressing in a suit, flashing your money around), the more likely that the locals will see or describe you as a 'gringo'. Most backpackers just revel in the term and are happy to describe themselves (and their fellow South American backpacker collective) as 'gringos'.

To Iguazu

Once New Year and the subsequent recovery period is over, it's time to move on once again. I pack what few belongings I have into my shitty new backpack; I can't even bear to give it a name. It weighs next to nothing, as I have very few belongings now. God, I miss Clive.

I try and drink lots of water and eat some fruit to put some goodness into my body; it feels as if I've been doing nothing but sitting on buses and getting drunk for months and months. On arrival at the bus terminal, all the nice looking and reputable bus companies are fully booked and I have to settle for one of the shabbier establishments. I grab a couple of *empanadas* (pastry turnovers filled with meat or cheese) and wait for my bus to pull up into the vast, docking bay at Buenos Aries station.

My bus shows up a little late and I'm extremely nervous and paranoid as I load my new bag into the hold (not that there's anything in there of any sentimental or monetary value any longer). I ensure that I'm given a receipt as advised, and stay outside the bus until the door is sealed on the hold. My luck with luxury buses has reached an abrupt end and, on entering I find that I'm cramped in next to an elderly woman with a persistent, chesty cough. She seems to distrust the baggage people even more than I do, as she's carried all of her belongings on board, taking up her foot space and most of mine.

It's a ridiculously long journey from BA to Iguazu, which is right up in the north of the country on the border with Brazil. The afternoon passes slowly and, as the night rolls in, I try and get some sleep to pass time, but it's difficult with the TV/DVD barking out a movie which I barely understand a word of and the coughing lady next door losing her lung. Early the next morning, around twelve hours into the journey, it becomes clear that there's something wrong with the bus. The air conditioning fails, and then the lights go (and fortunately with it the TV). We take a detour to the nearest depot and after the host explains what's happening (I have no idea what he said), we have to disembark and wait for a replacement bus.

An hour later, the replacement (which looks in a similar state of disrepair) shows up and within a few minutes of setting off, we find that this one has no air-conditioning to begin with (it's in the thirties outside) and there's an overpowering stench of urine to boot. I hold my nose and try and drop off to sleep; I'm awoken by a deep intake of breath and the sudden need to vomit when I hear shouting. From what I can make out, a chap has slept through his stop and is hurling abuse at the driver – blaming him for the misfortune. The bus stops and he gets off, still shouting, before walking round the back and throwing something into the engine. This, of course, causes another delay, whilst the driver, attendant and a gang of helpful passengers with various tools try to fix the problem.

We eventually arrive in Iguazu after more than twenty-two hours on the bus. I'm on tenterhooks as they unload the luggage but there it is! There's my $20 backpack! I catch a cab with an Israeli guy (who has also had all his stuff nicked in S.A) to a 'backpackers resort' which is something of a first; it looks as though 'Hostelling International' have taken over the ownership of an old holiday camp and geared it toward backpackers - a (filthy) pool, restaurant, bar and several huts populated with as many bunks as you can possibly squeeze in.

The following morning, I head to Parque Nacionales Iguazu. The bus that pulls up on the dry, dusty roadside outside the hostel is absolutely jam-packed, and people are hanging out of the door, so we squeeze five of us from the hostel into a cab instead. On entry to the park, I venture into the walking circuit around the falls, snatching brief, occasional glimpses, then all of a sudden there's a bloody great waterfall, and another - the biggest I've ever seen. It's hot, humid, sweaty stuff and awfully busy, I'm constantly trying to avoid the huge tour groups that are interfering with my relaxing day out.

Some of the views are simply amazing and the spray from standing close to the falls brings some welcome respite from the oppressive heat. I have a packed lunch at a cafe amongst some lizards that seem to have been tamed by the tourists and are munching on leftover food. After gathering my energy, I move out onto the upper circuit and see some phenomenal panoramic views of the falls, taking some great photos in the process. I'm losing a lot of fluids and getting sunburned so find some cover to take on some much needed liquid.

It's out into the sun once more to take a train toward the 'Garganta del Diablo' ('the Devils Throat'), having to walk along a metal catwalk over the river (worryingly there are workers fishing out what look to be old bit of catwalk from the river below). The Devils Throat is an awesome sight: straddling the borders of Argentina and Brazil, it's a huge, noisy, bubbling mess of a waterfall; a faint rainbow is suspended amongst the mass of spray. I can see the Brazilian side from here and wonder how easy it would be to cross. I'd say certain death was inevitable.

I take a big, yellow bus back to the hostel where a large BBQ party is promised. I part with some money and end up with a sausage and a small piece of chicken. After some complaints, the hostel lays on several buckets of *caipirinha* (Brazil's national cocktail), which seems to placate the crowd; it certainly placates me, I can't see.

27 - Chile

I spend a rain soaked week down in the Argentinean Lake District. Most of it stuck sheltering in a wood cabin which had a very strange 'orphanage-like' dorm set up, consisting of wooden shelves filled with mattresses. I have to spend money I can ill-afford on warm, waterproof clothes to allow me to spend time outdoors. Afterward, I take a bus across the Argentina-Chile border once more and we speed in the driving rain to a ramshackle town known as 'Puerto Montt'. As I begin my quest for some digs for the evening, a helpful, Dutch couple suggest a place that they've organised; as soon as I step foot in the reception I can see that even though it's not great it's far too clean and organised for my budget and make my excuses to go and search for a flea pit. I'm ushered into a rundown, graffiti covered hut and offered a cupboard there for a price that fits my budget, but am not really getting the feeling that I'll be safe so carry on my search until I find a family place that seems clean, friendly and not too much above what I can afford. The occasional English that one comes across in Argentina is long gone so it's 'speak Spanish or bust' now (normally bust). I have a quick look around the town and it seems as though someone has just emptied it out of a bin onto the side of a hill. There's a fairly unattractive promenade along the coastal front and an extremely oddball, enormous, multicoloured papiermache sculpture of a couple looking out to sea. I love it. I spend an enjoyable evening sitting in the kitchen of the guesthouse being taught some useful Spanish by one of the sons, whilst the ladies sit and play cards and hum along with the Spanish ballads playing on the radio in the background.

Hiking Alerce Andino – Flies

I have great trouble getting out of my nice warm bed in the morning, but when I discover that it's not raining outside, my mood improves. I'm headed for the 'Parque Nacional Alerce Andino', so I head down to the bus station to see what the best way to go about getting there is. I speak to a pretty, busty girl who explains where I need to catch the bus from before, searching half-heartedly for the bay and returning for another look to see if I had dreamt the size of her bosoms (I hadn't).

With some help from a chap who speaks a little English, I locate the bay and there sits a tiny little bus that's already packed. I squeeze on and we chug slowly along stony roads through the outlying villages. Suddenly, a truck speeds past the bus and slams on its brakes, causing the bus to screech to a halt (as an aside, the stopping distance for a bus travelling at two miles an hour is about a metre). A little old fellow jumps out of the renegade truck and hops onto the bus — an effective approach to overcome missing your bus I suppose. After many more stops, we arrive at the end of the line and the driver explains that it's a further three kilometre walk to the national park. On arrival at the park I have a brief chat with the park ranger who says a lot I don't understand and a little that I do. I gather that I need to leave my passport details and an emergency telephone number (of whom?). She explains that there's not enough time to make it to the lake I was planning on seeing, and directs me to a nice little woodland trail which winds upward along tracks still slippery from the rainfall, to a huge rock that looks over the surrounding woodland. I decide this is a fine spot to take lunch and remind oneself that it beats sitting at a desk (unless it's a desk on a huge rock overlooking woodland).

On arriving back at the warden's hut forty-five minutes later, I decide (stupidly, and against all advice) that there's every chance I can make it to the lake if I get a decent pace going — it's just nine kilometres and still only mid afternoon. I set off with great gusto and within seconds, am joined by a large, extremely annoying black fly (the size of a cat) which buzzes around my head loudly and doesn't seem to react at all to my waving it away, instead just easily dodging my frenzied swipes. I hatch a cunning plan which involves catching the fly unawares by sprinting away from him at speed - this seems to work quite well until I soon become short of breath and he catches up along with a couple of his equally keen-to-annoy mates. One fly was stressing me out, but a gang of three is far too much to handle, so I decide to throw the 'countryside code' out of the window and fight fire with fire by attacking them with an empty water bottle. I manage to down one and the bottle becomes my weapon of choice. Frustratingly, with each fly I wipe out, a replacement arrives. This is seriously damaging my chances of making it to the lake. There is one moment when I've got five of the bastards whizzing around my head and every time I swing my weapon they manage to move away. I panic, worried that they're some breed of super intelligent fly who've managed to figure out my technique and am about to slump to my knees in defeat and be devoured alive when, on my next wild swing with the bottle, I manage to strike down two with one blow. It becomes apparent that this epic battle has ended my hopes of making the lake and, with the light beginning to fade, I start to trudge back. The flies disappear with the light and I estimate that I've accounted for at least fifteen during the skirmish – hopefully they're not a protected species. Just as I'm cursing the length of the journey back, a jeep heads toward me and I hopefully thumb a lift – it transpires that the group of Germans (who look at me with concern at first, perhaps I still had my battle face on and was wielding a bottle angrily) are heading through Puerto Montt on their way home so I am saved both a long walk and an uncomfortable bus journey. It occurs to me that the warden may still be searching for me today – 'backpacker missing presumed eaten by gang of annoying giant killer flies'.

Puerto Varas

Half an hour's minibus journey away from Puerto Montt is Puerto Varas - a far more attractive town. The tourist office must lay claim to being one of the most picturesque ones in the world, situated at the beginning of a small pier out onto Lake Llanquihue, with the volcano Osorno way out on the far side of the lake. I muddle through a conversation with the girl at the tourist office and, after defining my accommodation requirements as 'very cheap', I am given directions to a *hospedaje* up the hill away from the lake. I take a stride upwards to the address where I am met in the street by a tiny old Chilean woman (Senora Carmen), who enquires as to whether I am the 'English boy' - the word is out in Puerto Varas. Senora Carmen leads me to a little, old wooden shack where I'm shown upstairs to a cosy box room in the roof (I feel a little like Heidi). The price is right so I accept. I look around the house and it reminds me of my nans old place, filled with trinkets and doilies and thirty years worth of carrier bags stashed in any available drawer. When the wind blows (or someone walks past at a brisk pace) the whole dwelling shakes. What follows is a surreal few days where the Senora seems to take me under her wing and give me some 'tough love'. I'm allowed a five-minute shower once a day (I opt for the evenings) and she lectures me on my poor Spanish (like I didn't know it was rubbish) in Spanish which means I can't understand what she's telling me off for most of the time anyway. I spend the days out walking in the nearby Parque Nacional Vicente Rosales and the evenings attempting to cook meals on Senora Carmen's 1920's coal powered stove which she hates me touching (I completely understand this, it would fetch a decent price on 'Antiques Roadshow'). She invariably takes over the preparation and cooking of all my food whilst I sit and watch Spanish soap operas.

Pucon

I'd told Senora Carmen that I had to leave and she locked me in a cupboard. I ended up escaping down the drainpipe under the cover of night as parts of the shack fell off around me. I travel North by bus to Pucon with the intention of climbing a volcano.

On arrival in the compact, touristy, yet attractive town, the weather is tremendously sunny and warm and the whole town has poured down onto the black sand (stone) beach by the huge lake. I join them for the afternoon and try to get my head around sitting on a beach with a great big volcano in my vision. I look forward to my quest to climb Volcano Villarrica the following day. Unfortunately, poor luck means that early the next morning the weather takes a turn for the worse and becomes exceedingly cloudy (which apparently means no volcano treks).

I arrange another attempt for the next morning and after shaking off a hangover I'd earned becoming acquainted with the other members of my hostel, set off on an extremely ambitious bike ride with two lads of a similar mindset to myself (idiots). With hindsight, four o'clock on a Saturday afternoon probably isn't the best time of day to embark on a forty-five kilometre cycle to yet another bloody lake, but accept the challenge we did and in great style, taking a wrong turn (possibly my fault – these people will keep listening to me) and getting lost in a national park - therefore turning a nice simple forty-five kilometre route into over sixty kilometres of leg-destroying hell. Sure, we found the lake eventually, but it was past eight o'clock at night, getting dark and beginning to rain. Cue the long, soul draining cycle home with no lights, in head on winds and driving rain - as you can imagine, spirits amongst the group were pretty high once we eventually made it back to the hostel, drenched and exhausted.

On Sunday morning, the rain continued relentlessly, the volcano trek was called off once more and I decided that I've seen enough trees, lakes and bikes for quite some time and head back northward toward Bolivia.

28 – Bolivia

It takes me several days and a string of tiring bus journeys to make my way up toward Bolivia. I sleep on the overnight buses and wash or (if I get lucky) shower in less-than-welcoming bathrooms in bus terminals. I spend my last day in Chile exploring the sun-baked streets of a somewhat rundown town – Valparaiso. I risk my life in the rusty *ascensors* (cliff-side lifts) and witness various stray dog fights before passing across into Argentina once more, catching an onward bus at Mendoza, keeping a frantic eye on what's left of my belongings the entire while. Finally, I decide to stop and recharge for a couple of days in Salta, up in Argentina's north and an overnight bus ride from the border with Bolivia.

After a couple of days re-acquainting myself with beds (albeit bunk beds), clean hot showers and Spanish spoken at a pace I can almost understand, I once again sample the fine Argentinean steak and wine, and spend some relaxed afternoons admiring the old Spanish architecture in warm, welcoming Salta. I've begun vomiting randomly and have a rash on my leg, so I take a trip to the pharmacist and, not being aware of any of the words for my symptoms, demonstrate by rolling up my trouser leg and propping it on the counter and making the universal sign language for being sick. Thankfully the patient lady behind the counter understands and gives me some pills and cream. Once I can cope with the concept of stepping onto a bus again I decide to bite the bullet and make for Bolivia tonight.

Border Crossing

I arrive at the Salta bus terminal and await the bus to La Quiaca, a town on the Argentinean side of the border. I see a 'well-travelled' bus chug in to the terminal and hope that this beaten-up wreck isn't going to pull into my bay which it duly does. My seat is in a great vantage position on the top deck and at the very front, which is as well, really, as I seem to have purchased a ticket for the only seat on the bus that doesn't recline. As the packed bus pulls off, all others around me tip their seats back and arrange themselves for the overnight trip whilst I sit bolt upright and look forward to eight hours of looking at utter darkness whilst sitting to attention.

Just before six in the morning, we pull into La Quiaca; it's pitch black and absolutely freezing. I dig out and wear all the warm clothes I have and trudge lonely through the dark, deserted streets toward the border crossing. I'm not overly comfortable with my surroundings and have got my wits about me, noticing a chap appear from a side street before sidling up behind and then beside me. I glance toward him and notice a scar across his face, he looks a fairly mean piece of work and I take a quick look about without letting on to see whether anyone else is around – they're not. He asks me the time and I tell him before he informs me that a) the border does not open for another two hours and b) he knows a way to get through now if I just follow him. He's joined by his buddy, a big chap with a severely smashed up nose, and they pause by an embankment, gesturing me to jump up and over after them. There's absolutely no way I'm following them but even with my paltry belongings, they're still heavy enough to be awkward and I'm not going to be able to make a run for it. I just thank them for their kind offer of sneaking through the border in the darkness, walk away, grimace and hope for the best. They call back after me but I make a good pace and, thankfully, they disappear.

After thanking my lucky stars that the situation didn't develop into anything nasty, I arrive at the border crossing and find that it opens at half past six. I join the waiting queue and after half an hour of sheltering from the cold, I'm walking into Bolivia and country number twenty-eight.

The town on the Bolivian side of the border - Villazon, is an absolute dive. Bolivia is a poor country, the poorest country in South America if I'm not mistaken (and there's every chance I am). It's an instantly visibly different world from Argentina and Chile. I spy a dead dog that looks like it's been lying in the gutter a fair while and locate the train station, intent on making my way Northward to Tupiza immediately. The station is closed so I take a breakfast of hot milk and goat's cheese at what may be a café (or could possibly just be someone's front room. They looked awfully surprised to see me).

When it becomes clear that the train station isn't going to be opening any time soon, I head back down the track to the chaotic bus terminal. In the melee I bump into a couple of young Aussie lads that I'd met in the hostel in Salta (and to be honest, didn't quite trust so had been trying to avoid) who seem pleased to see me, so we all buy a ticket for the same bus to Tupiza (hilariously they are relying on my Spanish skills). Whilst I'm waiting for the bus, I continue to marvel at how obviously different Bolivia is: the Bolivians are shorter in height, and have an 'American Indian' (I believe this is the PC description) like appearance with distinctive, sculpted faces. The women wear multi-coloured bright shawls, long, thick skirts and fantastic bowler hats adorned with flowers.

A hulking great monster-truck type bus with a raised chassis and massive tractor wheels shows up and I'm surprised to find the interior is more comfortable than I had expected. The journey is a rough one over gravel roads and at times it feels like being in a cement mixer. I'm so tired from having very little sleep over the last week and somehow drop off for a brief sleep in the blender. What seems like a couple of hours pass and we're dropped off on some dusty tracks on the outskirts of Tupiza - gateway to the barren, desolate Altiplano.

To the salt lakes! (Where it all went wrong)

Now, there is actually a very good reason for visiting the barren, desolate Altiplano of course. Along with the dizzyingly high altitude, freezing nights, complete lack of roads and mile after mile of nothingness, there are some positive traits - fantastic lakes (notably the worlds largest salt lake – the 'Salar de Uyuni'), hot springs, geysers, oh and llamas – we all know how brilliant they are.

It's wet season during our time here and heavy showers are regularly breaking out. We manage to find a ridiculously cheap room at a basic, but clean and friendly, hotel and lounge by the pool during the brief, hot & sunny intervals between frequent showers. Whilst we flip between sunbathing and sheltering, the rain is constantly flooding the hotel and giving the staff a real headache.

The tours out toward the salt lake are big business (in fact, other than accommodating those who come for the tours I'm pretty sure they're the towns only business) and after asking the advice of a few gringos who are on their way south, we choose and pay for one of the numerous 4x4 jeep tours on offer. Four days in a jeep, out to the middle of nowhere, with a guide and a cook - my kind of excursion!

On our way back to the hotel we carefully hop over the ever-growing puddles scattered around the muddy streets and are briefly held up from a cold beer by a pack of stray dogs out looking for trouble. We sacrifice one of the group and, whilst he's torn to shreds, we nip off to a nearby bar.

I sleep like a baby (in a cot) and awake to the sound of rain once more. The hotel is flooded again and we wade down to the entrance, skating on our flip-flops to where our 4x4 is being loaded. There's a short wait, so we saunter down to the nearby market to stock up on some more warm clothing and a little breakfast. I've been jealous of this whole 'women wearing bowler hats' malarkey and consider buying one myself; I'm put off by the incredulous look given to me by the chap manning the stall and buy some manly football socks instead.

The bags seem safely loaded onto the top of the jeep when we return and all is ready for the off. Along with myself and the two, young Aussie lads, there is a British couple as well, five passengers is just about comfortable in the vehicle. We make our way onward and upward and within hours, have reached 4000m above sea level, driving on narrow cliff-side roads with a great drop the other side. The altitude begins to affect me a little so I start chewing on coca leaves, which are supposed to help with altitude sickness. Lunch is taken from the boot of the jeep in the middle of nowhere with not a soul to be seen – quite an awesome feeling. There's a sticky moment in the afternoon, as the dirt roads are boggy from all the rain, and the jeep gets stuck in some waterlogged old tracks whilst driving upward on a cliff side. Our driver/guide and our cook (his father) jump into action and line the bog with ferns whilst we stand and watch, before carrying us on our merry way.

We reach our first night's accommodation just in time, as we pull into the remote village a huge thunderous storm moves in leaving us sheltered in little concrete huts, freezing cold and with the realisation that the warm clothes we'd purchased were not nearly enough for these conditions. And this my friends, is just about the point where it all went horribly wrong...

We had sat down to a dinner of chicken and chips and, although I had a bit of a dodgy stomach, I put it down to the high altitude and carried on tucking in. With not much available to entertain ourselves in an empty concrete shell, we retired to our dark, stony room for some sleep. I struggled to settle and found myself suffering from some pretty severe flatulence but again put both of these symptoms down to adjusting to altitude. Suddenly, with no warning, my mouth exploded with spittle and I knew that I had to get outside sharpish. I bounced around the darkened room toward the door and, with barely a second to spare, vomited violently as I fell out into the courtyard, hardly gaining my breath before the next surge of vomit arrives. I rest on my haunches and am sick a couple more times over the next twenty minutes. When I'm sure that there's nothing left inside me, I return to my bed, cold, soaking-wet and knackered. At least I manage to grab a couple of hours sleep.

I speak with my guide in the morning, trying to explain my symptoms with a mixture of 'Spanglish', sign language and a small dance of my own design. He digs out some pills for me, smiles and gives me a pat on the back. That's sorted then. Good.

We set off once more and, within minutes of being in the jeep, I realise that the magical pills haven't done the trick and things are worsening. I'm propped up against the open window, wrapped in every piece of clothing I can muster and sucking in the fresh air for dear life, but the need to vomit soon returns. I'm regularly screaming 'stop' to the guide so I can bundle from the vehicle and be ill. We climb up beyond 5000m and after another bout of vomiting (whilst the jeep and those within it sit patiently waiting), I slowly rise to my feet and am taken aback by the view of the lone track leading back though miles of snow dusted scrub toward white mountains way in the distance, I can honestly say I've never been sick in such beautiful surroundings.

Something of a snowstorm kicks off as we continue and, once it subsides, the surrounding craggy rock formations are covered with a layer of snow making for an amazing sight. The rest of the group is frolicking in the snow and I just about manage to crawl out of the jeep to take some photos of the scene before curling back up into a ball in my seat. A long day's driving draws to a close as we pull up beside some geysers but, by this point, I can hardly move and an attempt at peeling myself out of my seat is soon kyboshed by the intense cold.

I've never been so overjoyed to arrive anywhere as I am when we pull into the next village after the best part of twelve miserable hours cooped up in that jeep (miserable for me I mean, I'm sure everyone else was having a great time – apart from stopping every hour to watch me puke). Just when I think that things can't get any worse, I now have a bout of diarrhoea to cope with. My entire night is spent moving from my bed to the toilet/outside to be ill; I feel as though I'm on a 'liquid skewer' (sorry about painting that picture). After a sleepless night, I have an icy cold shower in the morning to try and make myself feel a little less horrible and pack my soiled clothes in several plastic bags. I'm unable to eat now; my body is rejecting everything within seconds of it reaching the back of my throat and all I'm able to do is drink water and chew coca leaves to try and help with the nausea. I'm really conscious that my condition is affecting others' enjoyment of the trip and this just stresses me out even further. I'm really beginning to worry now, we're still a couple of days away from civilization and I've got no idea what I've got, it seems a bit too grim for altitude sickness.

I've no choice but to get back into the jeep for another day of endless driving across barren lands with only llamas for company. We're shown many lagunas with varying features but I can't even get excited about flamingos (very unlike me). All I want to do is sleep and stop being sick. There are wonderfully shaped rocks that have been altered by the weather but I have no energy for hilarious photo opportunities – this must be serious. As we pull into the last overnight stop, we are joined by another tour group, and everyone is excited after being informed of the prospect of hot running water and alcohol. A hot shower makes me feel a little more human and I sit down to dinner with the rest of the group, managing to hold a conversation and force down a little food before having to sprint outside to vomit again minutes later. I finally get some sleep, curled up under a blissfully warm pile of heavy blankets. Hilarity ensues later in the night when I awake, bathed in sweat and in need of a toilet very soon. My room is pitch black and, as I feel my way toward the door, I trip on one of the lad's backpacks and crash onto the floor. I pick myself up in some pain and then have to navigate my way through a darkened dwelling to eventually fall onto the toilet and stay there for some time – what a mission.

The following morning brings a surprise. The guide, obviously concerned for my wellbeing, has arranged for a doctor to visit the village. I'm expecting some kind of witch doctor but it's just a regular chap in jeans and a t-shirt with a Red Cross medical kit. He takes my heart rate, informs me it's normal and comes to the conclusion that my stomach is full of acid. He gives me a few sachets of powder and buggers off. Another major development is that I'm able to eat something without it returning within seconds for the first time in three days. Things are looking up; it's also the last day in the jeep and we'll find ourselves in the closest thing you can find to civilisation in this part of Bolivia come this evening.

I definitely have a little more energy but want to make sure I have enough by the time we reach the salt lakes so am careful not to overdo things on the stops we make early in the day. We visit a valley of rocks that look like animals, a church and a train graveyard. Finally we reach the village that sits beside the 'Salar de Uyuni' – the crowning glory of the trip.

The few jeeps that were out in front of us slow down for the mandatory stop at the local stalls selling souvenirs made from salt and cactus. Our guide begins to slow, but we loudly urge him to continue toward the lake, promising that we'll stop on the way back. We pass the stationary vehicles and move out into the shallow water. It's like driving across a mirror: the sky, clouds and nearby mountains reflect onto the still water below with the brilliant white salt underneath.

After the best part of half an hour driving through the water, we pull up beside the 'salt hotel' (a shack made of salt sitting in the middle of the lake and home to some of the most hideous and pricey public toilets known to man). After removing our shoes, socks and rolling up the trouser legs, we jump down into the few centimetres of water that cover miles of salt and wander around in awe, taking in the spectacle. We manage to take some fantastic photos before any of the herds of sightseers have made their way across the lake. Once the crowds arrive, we take lunch out of the back of our jeep (with plenty of salt gags) before heading back across the lake. My fellow passengers ride up on the roof and marvel in the enormous mirror until we hit land again, whilst I enviously sit inside, wishing I was up there, all my energy spent on walking the lake.

We arrive in the town of Uyuni, which doesn't strike me as particularly hospitable, and the others begin to make plans to move on immediately. I'm in no fit state to be travelling anywhere, so I book a room for the night. I force some food down, buy several litres of water and collapse in a heap, wishing I was back safely at home more than any point on my travels.

To La Paz

I sleep well and once I wake decide that I can't stay cooped up in this room and the depressing Uyuni. After a few minutes of getting motivated, I struggle through some breakfast at an unhappy café before becoming embroiled in a pushing and shoving match at the train station to try and buy a ticket to Oruro overnight tonight, I'll then need to get a bus from Oruro to La Paz which is supposed to be easy enough. The energy it took to get my ticket has drained me again and I return to the guesthouse and pay to keep my room for the day. I spend the day sleeping, re-hydrating and on the toilet (although a lot less than I have been) between the occasional walk out to check that I haven't got the town wrong – I haven't, it's an unhappy sigh of a place. I walk around the local market but no one seems particularly keen on selling me anything.

At ten in the evening, I make my way through Uyuni's dark streets to the train station where there's absolutely nothing happening and the only place with any light is the foyer. I take a seat on the cold floor and am befriended by a blue and white dog. He's in a pretty bad state of repair, so I take pity on the poor bugger and give him a cookie; he turns his nose up at it and scuttles off. He attacks a couple of other strays nearing his turf before returning to lie by my side.

After an hour of sitting on the floor and steadily being joined by many more people taking up positions against the surrounding walls, the leader of a nearby tour group announces that the train is running four hours late, and will be leaving at four in the morning instead of midnight. I wander out into the cold air and the platform and utilize my ever-improving Spanish to ask one of the policemen/soldiers standing nearby whether he has any information. He informs me that two of the coaches that make up the train are here and they are awaiting the arrival of the remainder of the train. I notice that one of the coaches is the one I'm in so, rather than sit on the cold floor for another five hours, I clamber onboard the darkened carriage and join my Bolivian amigos for some sleep. I awaken just after four in the morning with the sound of another train arriving beside and shortly after some jolting and banging as (I assume) the coaches are joined together. I drift off again, content in the knowledge that next time I wake I'll be whizzing toward Oruro.

Driving rain against the carriage window awakens me again at six in the morning and, when I realise we're still sitting at the station, I panic and clamber off the train. The platform is empty and I run toward the building, extremely wary that I may have just spent the night in a disused carriage whilst my train came and went. Fortunately, the foyer is still full of tired, glum people and bags are still on trolleys waiting to go onto a coach that still hasn't arrived (although we're up to four now – where are they coming from?). The rest of the train eventually shows up half an hour later and, after a moving backwards and forwards session, the train finally moves away (backwards) at half past seven in the morning – Bolivia is certainly not predictable.

The journey drags terribly, seven hours seems to last for seven days. I flit between sleeping and cramping but am still overjoyed not to be vomiting or shitting. We finally reach Oruro and I've not got much energy left; I need to get on a bus to La Paz as soon as possible or I'm going to be stuck here. I'm not feeling great and bundle into a taxi with the tour guide I'd seen at the station in Uyuni. He asks if I'm OK and I explain (briefly) what's happened – when we get to the train station he steams through the mayhem of people selling tickets, into one of the offices and buys fifteen tickets to La Paz, making up the passenger names (FYI - I was Bill Cosby) handing me one and pointing out the bus I need to get on. The cramped bus takes around three and a half hours, eventually coming to a poor area on the outskirts (El Alto) and then alongside the huge crater which houses the sprawling city of La Paz - an amazing sight the first time you glimpse it. Buildings cling to the rim of the vast bowl and the rest of the city seems to have fallen into it. I'm not fussed with expense when I step off the bus and just get a cab into the city centre, finding a cheap cell with a hot shower and getting something to eat that isn't biscuits.

La Paz was just as rainy as the rest of my time in Bolivia and after taking another day trying to rehydrate and eat again, I popped my head out into another rainstorm, stepped into the ravines that run down the steep streets and jumped into a taxi to get set for another long bus journey across the border into Peru and Cusco.

29 – Peru

Machu Pichu

This was the part of South America I had been anticipating the most and am glad to say after a couple of days spent checking out the Inca walls and colonial architecture in the appealing old Inca capital of Cusco (as well as sheltering from the constant showers), my health had drastically improved, so my energy, enthusiasm for what remained of the journey and lust for life had returned in abundance.

I investigate the possibilities for making my way to Machu Picchu; when I arrived in South America I had my heart set on doing the 'Inca trail' which means several days trekking up to the ruins but with my recovery only days in and extremely limited availability on treks anyway I reluctantly (and sensibly for once) decide this is a non-starter. It seems my best (cheapest) option is to take a local bus out to a village called Olly-ammy-something-or-other and catch the late train from there.

After parting with the first of a fair bit of what little budget is left for the train ticket, I pick up my belongings and head for the local bus station (a shack with a yard). With luck, I manage to score a spot in the boot for my pack rather than loading it on the roof (I'm expecting rain any second) and retire to a wooden shed to have a bottle of the tooth-rotting 'Inca Cola' which is famous round these parts, whilst keeping an eye on my bag's whereabouts. When the time comes, I climb aboard the tiny bus (with horribly cramped seats and absolutely no leg room, resulting with me sitting with my chin between my knees). As we pull out of the parking area, we're surprisingly joined by the local magician who makes a tree out of a newspaper, strangles himself with a length of rope and makes a knot disappear from a shoelace before distributing boiled sweets, receiving a few donations of loose change for his performance and vanishing into thin air (jumping off the bus before it picks up speed).

As predicted, the rain doesn't take long to rear its head and the next two hours are spent staring out of the window at the mud and ever swelling rivers. We arrive in rainy Olly-ammy-something-or-other and hole up in a café to wait for the train. A train stops in on the way back to Cusco, and a gaggle of drenched, knackered looking backpackers file off. I witness all this through the window of the nice dry café whilst consuming a hot cup of tea and some apple pie and it's all very distressing.

The 'backpacker train' (so named because it's the cheapest option and is therefore full of backpackers) arrives and it's much nicer than imagined (I have just come from Bolivia) – spacious, clean and comfortable – they must invest some of the ticket money back into the trains. Its pitch black by now and the train is packed with chatty, excitable tourists. The river running alongside the train tracks sounds as if it's about to explode and burst its banks. Around an hour and a half later the train pulls into the final stop – Agua Calientes (Hot Water).

The backpackers steam off the train into the town centre in readiness to scrap for the accommodation that's on offer. I tag along with a couple I'd met in Cusco and the bloke, a French fellow, is adamant that he's going to find a guesthouse in 'Hot Water' with hot water (rumour has it this is quite a difficult task) so whilst he's off searching for some perfect rooms for us, we hole up in a bar and I have my first beer in quite some while – it tastes fantastic. The hot-water-seeking Frenchman returns shortly afterward with the news that all the best places are already full and, not wanting to tear ourselves away from the bar we're in to spend the evening hunting for accommodation, we pay for a couple of rooms upstairs which turn out to have no locks, graffiti on the walls and blankets nailed over the windows as curtains (I won't even go into the state of the bathroom). I hit the hay with everything crossed for a clear day tomorrow.

I awake at just before six in the morning, keen as mustard. 'Get in!' is the phrase heard on the pavements (there aren't really any streets) of Hot Water as I peel back the blanket-cum-curtain and find that the skies are-a-blue and it's pleasantly warm. We find that we're locked inside the bar and have to remove the slab of wood being used as a door to get outside. The river that runs beside the village is loud and angry, and it's from beside here that we catch another pricey tourist bus up toward the ruins. After some shenanigans at the entrance, which seems to be manned by an imposter who was pocketing the entrance fees, we stride upward toward the ruins, marveling at the great weather which is more fantastic than we could have hoped for - warm, sunny and hardly a cloud in the sky. We're feeling lucky but that must be nothing compared to the Inca trek groups who must feel like they're arriving in heaven after walking and camping in three days of relentless rain.

The sight you're confronted with the first time you set eyes on Machu Picchu is one of those 'always remember' moments. Shortly after drawing breath the next thought is 'how on earth did something like this get all the way up here'. It is, in short, the majestic, well-preserved ruins of an ancient Inca city built slap-bang on top of a mountain. My first thought is to get up higher for a better aerial view and, in all the excitement, I must have foolishly started trekking the Inca trail backward and after about a kilometre, realise that I'm walking further and further away from the ruins. I sheepishly head back and spend a good hour taking it all in, the city's buildings arranged across a flat green surface, the grassed terracing raising upward from there and way up, perched atop of a peak in the background, overlooking it all, is 'Waynu Picchu'. After the standard 'hey everybody! Look at me! I'm at Machu Picchu' photos, I wander down into the 'city centre' amongst the ruins and wonder at just how this could have been put together this high up; some of the stones used in the walls are absolutely massive. I can't take my eyes off Waynu Picchu in the distance and, seeing that some clouds are moving in; decide that if I missed out on the Inca trail, then the least I can do is drag my sorry body up the peak.

I knew that this was just the kind of dumbass stunt I thrive on, so sign a book at the base of the climb proclaiming that I was in perfect health to undertake a steep climb and gave my body some serious punishment as payback for what it put me through last week - that'll teach it. After an exhausting, hour climb and once I had stopped crying in agony, put my kneecaps back where they're supposed to sit and wiped the sweat/sun block mix from my eyes, I took in Machu Picchu all the way below. I clamber as high as you can possibly go, still mystified as to how they've managed to build a settlement on top of a peak that it's a nightmare just to climb up, let alone build stone buildings on – they must have had super Inca cranes. I just sit atop a rock, next to a couple sharing a spliff and a moment and take it all in.

After climbing/slipping/falling back down, I get that warm feeling you get when you've already completed something that the other people participating in are only half way along (like walking back down a marathon route with your medal round your neck and warm clothes on whilst others are still plodding to the finish). As I return to the entrance, a couple of people queuing take a look at my disheveled state and, after an exchange of glances, decide against the climb. I spend another hour or so walking the ruins as it begins to drizzle (it's quite welcome as it allows me to wash off the sweat and sun cream) and imagine what the buildings would have been used for during the Inca period. I was particularly impressed with the casino and spa complex. Way ahead of their time, them Incas.

The rain kicks in heavily again as I'm sitting on the bus waiting to head back down to Hot Water. I'm not fussed at all now, as I've done everything I wanted to and am happy to spend the remainder of the afternoon drinking coffee and people watching from under a café canopy. After fixing up a slightly more comfortable place to sleep (with hot water), I spend the evening at the hot springs. As I don't own any swim shorts due to the great coach robbery, I was considering inflicting my underwear on the general public but on reflection, decided no one deserved that and opted for a pair of football shorts. As it turned out, I needn't have bothered as some of the locals were parading a dazzling array of tanga briefs and big pants. Trying to put these nasty images aside, I concentrated on the sound of the nearby raging river, the surrounding peaks and the starry night sky. What an awesome day that was my friends - up there with the best of the trip.

29 and a half – Bolivia again

Fortunately, after spending the last couple of weeks at high altitude I'm getting quite used to it now, I can walk as far as twenty metres without collapsing into a wheezing heap. After returning to Cusco, I head downward to Lake Titicaca.

The lake spans the border of Peru and Bolivia (she's a big old girl). On the Peruvian side, you have the rather dull town of Puno which offers little more than the slightly oddball 'floating islands' - where a few hundred people live on islands built of bright yellow reeds (picture a big straw mattress), speak an old language rather than Spanish (just as I'm getting the hang of that) and make a living from selling handicrafts and rides in old longboats made out of reed to tourists visiting from the mainland. I have a feeling that this traditional lifestyle is something of a sham, as some of the huts have solar panels, and I'm almost certain I saw some kids gathered around a Playstation 2 complete with dance mat. The only other occurrence of note is my encountering a murderous hotel owner who tries to bump me off by over-polishing the wooden floors during the night in the hope that I will slip (which I do) and break my back (which I don't) - difficult to prove this motive.

Some three hours away across the border is the far cooler town of Copacabana. My arrival coincided with the annual fiesta, 'Fiesta de la Virgen de Candelaria'. The general idea is for each town to 'represent' with a big brass band, some dancing girls and a load of silly costumes before proceeding to dance and drink for 48 hours until the whole thing descends into a messy trail of crying women and brawling men. Marvellous stuff I'm sure you'll agree. I notice groups of girls dancing in extremely short skirts and stay a short while to ensure all is in order.

The main attraction from Copacabana is the 'Isla del Sol' which means 'Island de la Soul', and is named after an early nineties hip-hop group. Basically, someone has plonked Wales in the middle of a massive lake - Hilly, rocky, and windy and lots of sheep. You take a boat out there (it's actually the slowest boat in the world: I had to cut my toenails twice during the journey it took so long) and are dropped at the North of the island, you then walk four hours (I did it in three and a half because I'm awesome - an old man told me so) over a fairly testing trail to the South of the island. If you're clever (which I'm not) you realise there are only two villages, one at the beginning and one at the end and stock up on food/drink before you set off, and if you're a little backward (that'll be me then) you try and make the journey on a breakfast of 1 x snickers bar and have to be saved from the elements (and certain death) by a little girl selling you a banana on an isolated hilltop (what the hell is she doing out there on her own anyway?).

Strike!

I return to La Paz for a couple more days of sightseeing and then show up at La Paz airport at 7am on a Sunday morning to find that my chosen airline 'Lloyd Aereo Boliviano' (LAB) for my passage on to Brazil has decided to go on an 'indefinite strike'. The whole bleeding company! Not a single representative has come to work for four days (and counting) with little or no explanation. No customer service line, all the offices shut, check in desks completely unmanned - this could only happen in South America!

This leaves thousands of their passengers absolutely stranded with no guidance or source of advice whatsoever, scrambling to get onward/connecting flights with other companies and many a tearful women and raging man (and in some instances the reverse) fuming in the departure lounge.

After two further days stranded in La Paz formulating a plan, I join a determined, crack commando bunch of war veterans, escaped convicts and disgruntled backpackers back at the airport at five o'clock one morning. When it becomes clear that our friends at LAB aren't going to bother showing up again, we rush one of the check in desks and all bundle on a flight to anywhere. Our destination of choice turns out to be Santa Cruz, which although still in Bolivia, unlike La Paz, is warm, at sea level and a little more welcoming.

Whilst biding our time here until we can find an onward flight to Brazil, the desk guy at the guesthouse we are staying at gives us a tip about a nice country club out in the sticks where we can relax, have a swim and sunbathe. We decide to roll out there for the afternoon (passing some rather grand mansions with armed guards on the way - wonder who lives in those...). To cut a long story short, we end up being filmed for a Bolivian TV commercial (I starred as 'man with girlfriend') and receive payment in beer, which, although a little surprising, was most agreeable. I look forward to an influx of acting offers off the back of this, all of which hopefully involve payment in alcohol.

The La Paz escapees group all book onto the cheapest flight available into Brazil the next night (slightly worryingly with a company called 'goal'). I finally make it into a swamp in Brazil (Campo Grande) at three o'clock in the morning, five days later than planned, and shortly after manage to get straight on a flight to Rio (via Sao Paulo). I arrive in Rio tired, drained and seriously out of pocket and decide that's exactly where I'm going to stay until it's time to go home.

30 – Brazil

A night in Rio

I'd bedded in at a backpackers in the suburb of Botafogo, set in the gaze of the Christ the Redeemer statue up in the distance. I settle into a nice steady routine of hanging around the world-famous beaches of Ipanema and Copacabana during the day, impressing the locals with my samba football skills and then drinking at the hostel during the evening. I'd been told the key to keeping safe and out of bother in Rio is staying streetwise and haven't experienced any problems so far, however, a German fellow in the hostel refused to heed the advice and, instead of adopting the national dress of flip-flops, board shorts and vest, has decided to stick out like a sore thumb by wearing a loud Hawaiian shirt tucked into a pair of chinos. He manages to get mugged twice and witness a shooting in three memorable days.

Whilst I'm in Rio, the weather is constantly warm and humid, flipping between sun and showers. I had planned to make my way up to see the Christ statue at closer quarters on the afternoon of my second day, but decide to cancel as the sky begins to cloud over. A huge storm erupts and leaves a group of us who had planned a night out trapped inside the hostel eating pizza and drinking caipirinhas until we get the all clear at one in the morning – slightly worse for wear.

We head out to Lapa, a lively, raucous part of the city. We're just over a week away from Rio's world famous carnival and it looks like people are out practicing their moves (although this may be the case all the time). The noisy streets are packed with dancers and vendors selling beer out of large polystyrene coolers filled with ice. I try not to stick out like a sore thumb at first, but soon realise that no one really cares, so buy a couple of beers and soak up the unique atmosphere. We move with the crowd into a samba 'club' which seems to be a disused building; at the front of the house is a group of drummers accompanied by some 'ass shaking' female dancers who are being conducted behind a roped off area. Behind the rope, we are amongst a packed crowd of sweaty onlookers who are dancing at a frenzied pace as the rhythm of the drumming becomes faster and louder. These people are dancing as if they were possessed. I can't keep up with the pace and step out onto the street for a breath of fresh air, bathed in sweat. I have several drunken conversations with locals, I'm not sure how because I don't understand a word of Portuguese.

Our group moves onto a club; it's another sweaty affair, blasting out hip-hop at a volume that makes your ears bleed. There's one of those 'dance-off circles' going on and we're drunk enough to make ourselves look like idiots and join in. Our slick moves attract the attentions of four local girls and, as our luckless German friend is still fumbling a round of drinks onto the floor, that leaves a 'four on four' affair. Before I can even work out the logistics, the three Australian fellows I'm with have already moved in on the three girls that have teeth and the fourth, a toothless monster who looks like she's recently received a fierce electric shock, advances across the dance floor toward me with lust in her eyes. I scream and run for dear life out to the street, diving into the nearest taxi and finding I'm too drunk to remember where I live. The driver reels off a list of suburbs and when I hear one I recognise, I shout loudly. Somehow I make it home as the sun is coming up and, when I awake in the mid-afternoon, I discover that caiprinihas have a degenerative effect and I'm more hammered than I was when I fell into bed.

The Maracana

There was one place in Rio I was particularly looking forward to seeing. You can have your fill of beaches and beautiful girls at many of the places I've visited on this trip but ever since I began my lifelong obsession with football, I've wanted to visit the magnificent Maracana football stadium, home of the Brazilian national side, as well as four Rio club sides - arguably the most magical stadium in the world.

As luck would have it (about time I got a slice of that), my temporary home of Botafogo has a team that has made it to the state final - which takes place on this very day at the stadium. The game is a sell-out (The Maracana was undergoing major renovation for the Pan-American games so the capacity had been lowered), but a small group of football fans from the hostel take a trip down to the ground in the hope of getting hold of some tickets. I marvel at the manic goings on outside the ground - street beer vendors everywhere you look, a guy walking around with a bottle of tequila and a tray of limes and salt selling pre-match shots, inter-gang scuffles and random muggings of ticket touts along with the mandatory football songs. I should be on edge with all this happening, but after a couple of beers, I'm happy just to soak up the atmosphere. I purchase a counterfeit shirt of my new favourite side and enter the stadium, striding up the concrete ramp towards a cacophony of noise. Anyone who goes to football will know the feeling you get when you first walk into a stadium and glimpse the green playing arena, it's a great rush – particularly when it's a ground that you've always wanted to visit.

The seats are all full and there is barely standing room. Men and children are crammed in anywhere there is a space and even the raised concrete sides of the tunnels are being utilised as vantage points. We have to make do with squeezing into one of the walkways alongside countless others. Looking out over the stadium, Botafogo has 80% of the crowd and the atmosphere is incredible. Tens of thousands of supporters dressed in black and white, with huge flags and drums, constantly singing and dancing as drizzle falls. It only takes another couple of the local brews and I'm in amongst them, joining in, my allegiance decided. One of the lads from the hostel has made the mistake of donning a t-shirt in the opposition's colour of red, and some of the locals take exception to this, ordering him to remove it immediately and then laughing when his embarrassment causes his face to glow red and they order him to remove that as well. 'Fogo' go in at half time 1-0 down but on returning to the sodden pitch fifteen minutes later are roused by an ear-splitting song from their passionate fans (no idea what the words were - I just shouted a few choice English swear words combined with 'when the saints go marching in') which raises the roof and gets their players playing some decent football. Three second-half 'Fogo' goals, a sending off for the opposition, fireworks, sparklers, more sing/dance-a-longs and being hugged by a group of big, half-naked, sweaty Brazilian dudes were my second half highlights and led to Botafogo (us) becoming state champions and the beginning of some major street parties (although probably not by Brazilian standards) - a cracking day at the football.

With only a couple of days left until my flight back to London, I manage to cram in a few of the 'must see' tourist sights around the city. Firstly I finally manage to visit the famous 'Christ the redeemer' statue that peers over the immense city. As I stare up quizzically at a nice, big statue base surrounded by cloud, thinking the morning would have been better spent at the beach, the man himself finally appears, framed by deep blue sky and cutting a formidable figure – a magical moment indeed. I'm not so lucky with the weather when taking the cable car up to the Sugarloaf Mountain however; I find it's so misty that I couldn't even see my feet, let alone any of the views.

On the morning of my departure, I buy as many pairs of bargain flip-flops as I can afford and bid farewell to Rio. I walk down to the manic main street to take my last bus trip of the trip (thank God) to the airport; an unsuccessful hour of crossing the aforementioned street several times trying to find a bus that goes to the airport follows (and once again neutralising the purpose of my pre-flight shower). I give up and blow every penny I have remaining on a taxi.

What happened next

As I sit in the departure lounge at Rio, I can say unequivocally that I never want to sleep in a bunk bed or in a dormitory surrounded by strangers ever again. I want to shower in a cubicle where the plughole isn't blocked with a mass of assorted pubic hair, I want to put my food in a fridge and know that when I come to eat it the following morning it hasn't become someone's drunken midnight snack. I want a long, hot, deep bath and I want to eat something that isn't pasta or noodles. I don't want to tell anyone who I am, where I'm from and where I've been. I'd like to be left to my own devices for a couple of days. I want to see a familiar face. I don't plan to set foot on a bus or a plane for a very long time (other than the one I'm waiting for of course, I don't plan on staying in the departure lounge).

The first few days of being back home from traveling are wonderful. There's a warm welcome from the family and seemingly endless catching up with friends. Everyone you bump into is keen to hear your stories and ask of your favourite place. Old haunts that had gone stale now feel fresh again. Home comforts never felt so comforting and it genuinely feels good to be home. There's even a contented sigh and a little smile when local youths pepper train goers with bottles on a Friday night – England, my England.

Then normality and routine suddenly kick in. You find yourself in the same old places that you were sick of when you left, friends lose interest in your hilarious anecdotes within a couple of weeks and revert to talk of jobs and houses. Being confronted by a gang of dribbling, feral teenagers just isn't as entertaining as it once was; even folks that you met on the road who were 'kindred spirits' and 'lifelong friends' just seem to disappear by the wayside with time. Money needs to be earned to survive; a job needs to be found.

Fast forward eighteen months and I find myself sat staring at a screen again, mind-numbingly bored, staring up at pictures placed there to remind me of more inspiring times and counting down the hours until the weekend arrives. There's no longer the question of 'there must be more to life than this?' because you know there is, so much more; you've experienced it and there's nothing that can beat the knowledge that each day you have the ability to wake and set off for somewhere you've never been before, to encounter someone you've never met, with the knowledge that absolutely anything can happen.

Suddenly bunk beds don't seem such a bad idea…